101 Easy
Reading Games
Grade 2

by Becky Daniel-White

Published by
Frank Schaffer Publications®

Author: Becky Daniel-White
Editors: Kim Bradford, Mary Hassinger

Frank Schaffer Publications ®

Send all inquiries to:
Frank Schaffer Publications
8720 Orion Place
Columbus, Ohio 43240-2111

101 Easy Reading Games—grade 2
ISBN: 0-7682-3412-3

1 2 3 4 5 6 7 8 9 MAZ 11 10 09 08 07 06

Table of Contents

Introduction

Games are a fantastic way to teach and reinforce concepts in students of all ages. The problem with many educational games is that they are too complicated and time consuming to set up and learn. They require hours of teacher preparation and lengthy explanations to students. Something that is supposed to be fun turns out to require a lot of work.

This book addresses that problem by patterning reading games after familiar and well-loved game types, such as Bingo and Memory. By building on students' prior knowledge of game structure and rules, time can be spent actually playing the games and reinforcing target concepts.

101 Easy Reading Games is broken down into 10 major sections, according to game category. Game boards and activity pages are included with the game instructions, and cards are conveniently grouped at the back of the book. These materials and ideas will provide you and your students with hour upon hour of fun reading practice!

There are games in this book addressing all five of the key Reading First skills: phonemic awareness, decoding, fluency, vocabulary, and comprehension. You will find the games indexed by these skills on page 128.

You will find that *101 Easy Reading Games* will provide you and your students with many hours of reading fun!

Published by Frank Schaffer Publications.
Copyright protected.

0-7682-3412-3
101 Easy Reading Games

Hangman Games

Any of the Hangman games in this section can be played two ways. The first way is like traditional hangman and hangman-type games. A word or phrase is chosen and represented on a board or paper with one blank for each letter. The player who chose the word and knows the answer fills in the blanks with letters as the other players guess them. Incorrect answers are penalized by adding on one body part at a time to the "hangman." The object of the game is for players to guess the word or phrase before the complete hangman is drawn. The person who guesses the correct answer then takes a turn choosing the word and filling in the blanks. Any object may replace the "hangman," as long as there are a designated number of parts that make up a finished object (e.g., a jack-o-lantern face at Halloween time, a cat for short a words, a house for settings, etc.).

The second way to play these Hangman games is Reverse Hangman. This version is played exactly like the first version, with one exception. Instead of adding parts to make a complete picture, players in Reverse Hangman begin with a complete picture and have one part erased for each incorrect letter guess.

For each game you play, decide ahead of time which way you are going to play, and what type of "hangman" figure you are going to use. Then have fun as you reinforce all sorts of reading concepts!

 **Number Word Hangman**

Objective: build fluency with basic number words

Materials: Number Word cards (page 103); chart paper, overhead projector, or white board to write on

Getting Ready: Reproduce and cut apart the word cards. Place them in a large box or bag.

Setting: Students gather at the board.

How to Play:
1. One player is chosen to go first and draws a word.
2. The player who drew the word represents it on the board with one blank line for each letter.
3. Play proceeds according to standard Hangman rules.
4. The first student to correctly guess the word is then in charge of choosing and drawing blanks for the next word. Play continues this way until you choose to stop playing.

Hangman Games

2 Hangman with Sight Words and Other Common Words

Objective: build fluency with sight words, food words, animal words, and other common grade-appropriate words

Materials: one set of word cards (choose any set of cards from pages 106–115); chart paper, overhead projector, or white board to write on

Getting Ready: Reproduce and cut apart the word cards. Place them in a large box or bag.

Setting: Students gather at the board.

How to Play:
1. One player is chosen to go first and draws a word.
2. The player who drew the word represents it on the board with one blank line for each letter.
3. Play proceeds according to standard Hangman rules.
4. The first student to correctly guess the word is then in charge of choosing and drawing blanks for the next word. Play continues this way until you choose to stop playing.

3 Hangman with Compound Words

Objective: develop vocabulary and fluency with compound words

Materials: Compound Word cards (page 119); chart paper, overhead projector, or white board to write on

Getting Ready: Reproduce and cut apart the word cards. Place them in a large box or bag.

Setting: Students gather at the board.

How to Play:
1. One player is chosen to go first, draws a word, and represents it on the board with one blank line for each letter.
2. Play proceeds according to standard Hangman rules.
3. The first student to correctly guess the word must come up to the board and circle the two separate words that make up the compound word. If she correctly identifies the two words, she repeats the process with the next word.

Alternate Version: Instead of using the cards above, use the Compound Word Riddles cards from page 120. The player draws a card, reads the riddle aloud, and uses blanks as usual to represent the word in parentheses at the bottom of the card. Play then proceeds as usual until the word is guessed.

Published by Frank Schaffer Publications.
Copyright protected.

0-7682-3412-3
101 Easy Reading Games

Hangman Games

 4 ## Hangman with Synonyms or Antonyms

Objective: develop vocabulary and build fluency with antonyms

Materials: Synonym cards (page 117) and/or Antonym cards (page 118); chart paper, overhead projector, or white board to write on

Getting Ready: Reproduce and cut apart the word cards. Place them in a large box or bag.

Setting: Students gather at the board.

How to Play:
1. One player is chosen to go first and draws a word.
2. The player who drew the word pair chooses one of the words and represents it on the board with one blank line for each letter.

3. Before accepting letter guesses, the player says, "This word is the antonym (or synonym) of ___," and reads the other word off the card.
4. Play proceeds according to standard Hangman rules.
5. The first student to correctly guess the word repeats the process with the next word.

Alternate Version: Play Hangman with other categories of vocabulary words, such as synonyms, contractions, plurals, and homophones. You may use appropriate cards from pages 120 and 121 to play, with the word or words in parentheses as the mystery word(s). Read the clue before taking letter guesses, then proceed according to standard Hangman rules.

 5 ## Spelling Word Hangman

Objective: develop reading and spelling skills with current spelling words

Materials: a list of your class's spelling words; chart paper, overhead projector, or white board to write on

Getting Ready: Write spelling words on pieces of paper to make word cards. Place them in a large box or bag.

Setting: Students gather at the board.

How to Play:
1. One player is chosen to go first, draws a word, and represents it on the board with one blank line for each letter.
2. Before accepting letter guesses, the player must use the word in a sentence.
3. Play proceeds according to standard Hangman rules.
4. The first student to correctly guess the word must use it correctly in another sentence. If she uses it correctly, she repeats the process with the next word.

Alternate Version: Instead of using the spelling word in a sentence, you may have players define each word, draw it, give a synonym or homonym, or act it out.

Hangman Games

6 Story Element Hangman

Objective: develop ability to identify basic story elements: characters, setting, problem, solution, and events

Materials: Story Element graphic organizer (page 9); chart paper, overhead projector, or white board to write on

Getting Ready:

1. Copy one Story Element graphic organizer for each student in your class.
2. Pass out the graphic organizers. Students choose a book or story they are familiar with and fill in the spaces with the correct information (i.e., characters, setting, problem, solution, and events).
3. When everyone is finished filling out their graphic organizers, collect all the pages, fold them, and place them in a large box or bag.

Setting: Students gather at the board.

How to Play:

1. Choose a specific element to focus on or allow each student to choose which element he is going to use.
2. One player is chosen to go first and draws a graphic organizer out of the box.
3. The player at the board writes blanks to represent his choice (e.g., __ __ __ __ __ to represent *a farm* as the setting for "The Little Red Hen").
4. Before accepting letter guesses, the player must share which story element he used.
5. Play proceeds according to standard Hangman rules.
6. The first student to guess the correct answer must then identify the title of the story or book. If she identifies it correctly, she repeats the process with the next element.

Published by Frank Schaffer Publications.
Copyright protected.

0-7682-3412-3
101 Easy Reading Games

Story Element Graphic Organizer

Characters	Setting

Problem	Solution

Beginning Events	Middle Events	Ending Events

Published by Frank Schaffer Publications.
Copyright protected.

0-7682-3412-3
101 Easy Reading Games

Hangman Games

7 Cause and Effect Hangman

Objective: demonstrate ability to generate and identify corresponding causes and effects

Materials: Cause and Effect graphic organizer (see below); chart paper, overhead projector, or white board to write on

Getting Ready:
1. Copy one Cause and Effect graphic organizer for each student in your class.
2. Pass out the graphic organizers. Students make up a set of corresponding causes and effects.
3. When everyone is finished filling out their graphic organizers, collect all the pages, fold them, and place them in a large box or bag.

Setting: Students gather at the board.

How to Play:
1. One player is chosen to go first and draws a graphic organizer out of the box.
2. The player represents either the cause or the effect on the board with one blank line for each letter in the sentence.

3. Before accepting letter guesses, the player must read the other sentence on the paper aloud and identify it as the cause or effect. (e.g., "The effect is 'School was canceled.' What is the cause?")
4. Play proceeds according to standard Hangman rules.
5. The first student to correctly guess the complete mystery sentence is then in charge of choosing and drawing blanks for the next word. Play continues this way until you choose to stop playing.

Alternate Version: Instead of having students create their own cause and effect cards, you may use the cards from page 126 or the sentences on the What If cards (page 125). You may also ask the student who correctly identifies the mystery sentence to give an alternate cause or effect before being allowed to draw a new card and continue play.

Cause and Effect Graphic Organizer

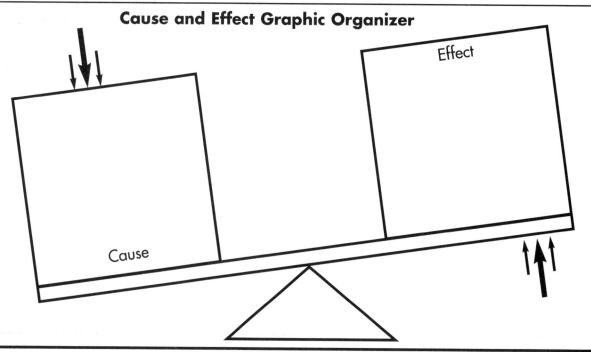

Published by Frank Schaffer Publications.
Copyright protected.

0-7682-3412-3
101 Easy Reading Games

Hangman Games

 **Fact and Opinion Hangman**

Objective: demonstrate ability to generate facts and opinions, and correctly identify statements as facts or opinions

Materials: Fact and Opinion graphic organizer (see below); chart paper, overhead projector, or white board to write on

Getting Ready:
1. Copy one Fact and Opinion graphic organizer for each student in your class.
2. Pass out the graphic organizers. Students think of and write one fact and one opinion.
3. When everyone is finished filling out their graphic organizers, collect all the pages, fold them and place them in a large box or bag.

Setting: Students gather at the board.

How to Play:
1. One player is chosen to go first and draws a graphic organizer out of the box.
2. The player who drew the paper represents either the fact or opinion on the board with one blank line for each letter in the sentence.
3. Play proceeds according to standard Hangman rules.
4. The first student to correctly guess the complete mystery sentence must then identify whether the statement is a fact or an opinion. If she correctly identifies it, she is then in charge of choosing and drawing blanks for the next fact or opinion. Play continues this way until you choose to stop playing.

Fact and Opinion Graphic Organizer

Fact	Opinion

Hangman Games

 **Fantasy or Reality Hangman**

Objective: demonstrate ability to distinguish between fantasy and reality and to correctly identify stories as fantasy or reality

Materials: pieces of plain paper or scrap paper; chart paper, overhead projector, or white board to write on

Getting Ready:
1. Pass out the small pieces of plain or scrap paper. Students think of and write one story title, and the word *fantasy* or *reality* to correctly identify the type of story it is.
2. When everyone is finished filling out their papers, collect them, fold them, and place them in a large box or bag.

Setting: Students gather at the board.

How to Play:
1. One player is chosen to go first and draws a story title out of the box.
2. The player who drew the paper represents the title on the board with one blank line for each letter in the sentence.
3. Play proceeds according to standard Hangman rules.

4. The first student to correctly guess the complete mystery sentence must then identify whether the story is fantasy or reality. If she correctly identifies it, she is then in charge of choosing and drawing blanks for the next fact or opinion. Play continues this way until you choose to stop playing.

Alternate Versions:
A. You may choose to reveal whether the story is fantasy or reality before taking letter guesses. This will inform everyone's story guesses and get them to think about the stories that fit a certain type. Once the title has been guessed, the player who guessed it must give two or three reasons why the story is either fantasy or reality (e.g., imaginary or no imaginary characters, animals that do or do not talk, realistic or imaginary setting, and so on).
B. You may play Fiction or Nonfiction Hangman the same way as the game above, using the categories of fiction and nonfiction instead of reality and fantasy.

Published by Frank Schaffer Publications.
Copyright protected.

0-7682-3412-3
101 Easy Reading Games

Hangman Games

Classification Hangman (Main Idea & Details)

Objective: demonstrate ability to determine a main idea from a given set of details

Materials: Main Idea & Details graphic organizer (see below); chart paper, overhead projector, or white board to write on

Getting Ready:

1. Copy one Main Idea & Details graphic organizer for each student in your class.
2. Pass out the graphic organizers. Students think of and write one main idea or category and three corresponding details or items. (For example, Insects: flies, ants, beetles; I am healthy: I eat good food; I exercise; I am not sick.)
3. When everyone is finished filling out their graphic organizers, collect all the papers, fold them, and place them in a large box or bag.

Setting: Students gather at the board.

How to Play:

1. One player is chosen to go first and draws a graphic organizer out of the box.
2. The player who drew the paper represents either the main idea or detail on the board with one blank line for each letter.

3. Before accepting letter guesses, the player must read aloud the details listed on the paper. (e.g., "The details are *frozen, water,* and *flakes.* What is the main idea?")
4. Play proceeds according to standard Hangman rules.
5. The first student to correctly guess the main idea is then in charge of choosing and drawing blanks for the next main idea. Play continues this way until you choose to stop playing.

Alternate Versions:

A. Instead of creating your own main idea and detail statements, you may use the main ideas and details from the "classify" cards on page 127. Reproduce and cut them apart, then place them in a box or bag. Proceed with Hangman as above.
B. The player at the board may list the details with blanks and state the main idea before taking letter guesses.
C. Players may list the details on the board with blanks and withhold the main idea. The first player to correctly guess the details listed must then correctly identify the main idea before taking a turn as the writer.

Main Idea & Details Graphic Organizer

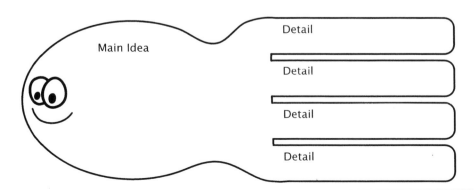

Hangman Games

11 Black Widow Hangman

Objective: introduce and reinforce words that begin with "bl"

Materials: index cards, marker, paper bag, white board (or overhead, chalkboard, or chart paper)

Getting Ready:

1. On index cards, print the following words: *ack, ade, ame, and, ank, are, aze, eak, eat, end, ess, ind, iss, ock, ond, ot, ow, ue, uff, ur, urt,* and *ush.*
2. Place the letter cards in a paper bag.

Setting: Students gather at the board.

How to Play:

1. Divide students into three or four teams.

2. The first player draws a large spider with eight legs on the board. Next, he draws a card from the bag. He uses those letters plus the "bl" blend to make a word. Then he is to give verbal hints to convey the word to team members (e.g., for *blow,* he could say "the wind does this").

3. Team members take turns guessing. Each time a team member guesses incorrectly, the player has to erase one of the spider's legs.

4. When someone on the team names the word, the team gets as many points as there are legs left on the spider.

5. As you play, keep score on the board.

6. After everyone has had a turn, total the points to see which team won.

12 The Fly Flies Hangman

Objective: introduce and reinforce words that begin with "fl"

Materials: white board (or overhead, chalkboard, or chart paper)

Getting Ready: On the board, draw a simple fly. Begin with a body and add twelve parts—six legs, two wings, and two antenna.

Setting: Students gather at the board.

How to Play: Play as Black Widow Hangman, but with "fl" words and ten fly parts instead of eight spider parts.

13 Seven Guesses Hangman

Objective: introduce and reinforce words that begin with "sh"

Materials: white board (or overhead, chalkboard, or chart paper)

Setting: Students gather at the board.

How to Play: Play according to standard Hangman rules, but give players only seven guesses. If they guess correctly within seven guesses, the class gets a point. If not, the teacher gets the point.

Published by Frank Schaffer Publications.
Copyright protected.

0-7682-3412-3
101 Easy Reading Games

Memory

Play the games in this section like traditional memory, with cards set up facedown in a grid. Players play to see who can make the most matches.

 **"BR" Word Match**

Objective: introduce and reinforce words that begin with the "br" blend

Materials: "BR" cards (pages 89–90), cardstock, paper cutter, rubber bands

Getting Ready:
1. Reproduce a set of "BR" cards for each student.
2. Cut apart the cards and secure each deck with a rubber band.

Setting: Two to four players work on a flat surface, such as a floor or table.

How to Play:
1. Use the cards to play Memory. First, players place the 40 cards facedown in eight rows of five cards.
2. Players take turns flipping over a pair in an attempt to match a clue card with the correct "br" word.
3. If a player turns over two cards that are not a match, she lays them facedown again.

4. When one player finds a match, she must correctly read the "br" word aloud to keep the pair of cards. If she does not read it correctly, the match must be flipped back over, and play passes back to the other player.
5. The player with the most cards at the end is declared the winner.

Alternate Versions:
A. Instead of having students match "br" words with pictures, have two players combine sets of word cards with the clue cards removed. Players must match the two identical words.
B. Have each student shuffle his deck of cards. See how many matches he can make in three minutes.
C. Have students glue corresponding words and pictures back to back to make flashcards for practicing the "br" words.

Memory

15 "FR" Word Match

Objective: introduce and reinforce 20 words that begin with the "fr" blend

Materials: "FR" cards (pages 91–92), cardstock, paper cutter, rubber bands

Getting Ready:
1. Reproduce a set of "FR" cards for each student.
2. Cut apart the cards and secure each deck with a rubber band.

Setting: Two to four players work on a flat surface, such as a floor or table.

How to Play:
1. Use the cards to play Memory. First, players place the 40 cards facedown in eight rows of five cards.
2. Players take turns flipping over a pair in an attempt to match a picture card with the correct "fr" word.
3. If a player turns over two cards that are not a match, she lays them facedown again.
4. When one player finds a match, she must correctly read the word aloud to keep the pair of cards. If she does not read it correctly, the match must be flipped back over, and play passes back to the other player.
5. The player with the most cards at the end is declared the winner.

Memory

16 Other Decoding Word Match Games

Objective: introduce and reinforce words with specific blends: "gr," "tr," "sm," "sn," "sk," "sp," "sq," "st," "sw" and "ng"

Materials: sturdy cardstock, paper cutter, any type of word cards (pages 96–101, see list below)

Word Cards for Use with Decoding Memory
"GR" Cards (93)
"TR" Cards (94)
"CR" Cards (95)
"PL" Cards (96)
"SL" Cards (97)
"SM" and "SN" Cards (98)
"SK," "SP," "SQ," "ST," and "SW" Cards (99–100)
"NG" Cards (101)

Getting Ready:
1. Reproduce the chosen set or sets of cards for each student.

2. Cut apart the cards and secure each deck with a rubber band.

Setting: Two to four players work on a flat surface, such as a floor or table.

How to Play:
1. Use the cards to play Memory. First, players combine two sets of cards and place them facedown in several rows and columns.
2. Players take turns flipping over a pair in an attempt to match identical words.
3. If a player turns over two cards that are not a match, she lays them facedown again.
4. When one player finds a match, she must correctly read the word aloud to keep the pair of cards. If she does not read it correctly, the match must be flipped back over, and play passes back to the other player.
5. The player with the most cards at the end is declared the winner.

17 Number Word Match

Objective: introduce and reinforce basic number words zero through twenty, as well as thirty, forty, fifty, sixty, seventy, eighty, and ninety

Materials: Number Word cards (page 103), paper cutter, rubber bands

Getting Ready:
1. Reproduce a set of cards for each student.
2. Cut apart the cards and secure them with a rubber band.
3. Give each student a set of cards and review words together.

Setting: Two to four players work on a flat surface, such as a floor or table.

How to Play:
Have students pair up, mix two sets of cards together, and play Memory with the combined set. They are to take turns turning over two cards to find word matches. When they find a match, they must correctly read the word to keep it. If they cannot correctly read the word, the match must be turned back over, and play passes back to the other player.

18 Animal Word Match

Objective: introduce and reinforce animal words

Materials: Animal Word cards (pages 106–107), paper cutter, rubber bands

Getting Ready:
1. Reproduce a set of cards for each student.
2. Cut apart the cards and secure them with a rubber band.
3. Give each student a set of cards, and review the words together.

Setting: Two to four players work on a flat surface, such as a floor or table.

How to Play:
Have students pair up, mix two sets of cards together, and play Memory with the combined set. They are to take turns turning over two cards to find word matches. When they find a match, they must correctly read the word to keep it. If they cannot correctly read the word, the match must be turned back over, and play passes back to the other player.

Alternate Version: Instead of having students match two identical animal words, give half of the students sets of Animal Picture cards (pages 104–105). Players must match words with the correct pictures.

19 Food Word Match

Objective: introduce and reinforce food words

Materials: Food Word cards (pages 110–111), paper cutter, rubber bands

Getting Ready:
1. Reproduce a set of cards for each student.
2. Cut apart the cards and secure them with a rubber band.
3. Give each student a set of cards, and review the words together.

Setting: Two to four players work on a flat surface, such as a floor or table.

How to Play:
Have students pair up, mix two sets of cards together, and play Memory with the combined set. They are to take turns turning over two cards to find word matches. When they find a match, they must correctly read the word to keep it. If they cannot correctly read the word, the match must be turned back over, and play passes back to the other player.

Alternate Version: Instead of having students match two identical food words, give half of the students sets of Food Picture cards (pages 108–109). Players must match words with the correct pictures.

Memory

 **Sight Words**

Objective: practice reading sight words

Materials: Sight Word cards (pages 112–115), paper cutter, rubber bands

Getting Ready:
1. Reproduce a set of cards for each student.
2. Cut apart the cards and secure them with a rubber band.
3. Give each student a set of cards. If you wish, review the words together (see list below).

Setting: Two to four players work on a flat surface, such as a floor or table.

How to Play:
1. Have students pair up and choose 20 words from one set of cards. Find those same 20 cards in the other deck and shuffle the 40 cards together facedown.
2. Students set up cards facedown in five rows of eight and play Memory with the combined set. They are to take turns turning over two cards to find word matches. When one player finds a match, he must correctly read the word to keep it. If he cannot correctly read the word, the match must be turned back over, and play passes back to the other player. Repeat play with the same set or different words.

Here is the complete list of the sight words from the cards.

Sight Words

about	afterward	against	always	anyone	around
because	been	before	best	better	both
bring	caller	came	carry	clean	cold
come	could	does	done	down	draw
drinking	everyone	falling	faster	finding	first
found	four	from	full	funny	gave
give	goes	going	good	grow	have
help	here	him	holding	hurt	into
its	jumping	just	keep	kind	knew
knight	laugh	light	little	long	look
made	make	many	much	must	myself
never	new	nothing	now	off	older
once	only	open	ourselves	out	over
own	player	please	pick	pretty	pulling
putting	read	right	round	said	seesaw
saying	seven	shall	she	show	sing
sleep	small	some	soon	start	student
take	teacher	thank	that	the	their
them	then	there	these	they	think
this	today	together	tomorrow	try	under
upon	use	very	walk	want	warm
was	wash	well	went	were	what
when	where	willing	wish	with	worker
would	writer	yes	you	your	zoo

21 Homophone Match

Objective: introduce and reinforce compound words

Materials: Homophone cards (page 116), paper cutter, rubber bands

Getting Ready:
1. Reproduce a set of cards for each student.
2. Cut apart the cards and secure them with a rubber band.
3. Give each student a set of cards, and review the words together.

Setting: Two to four players work on a flat surface, such as a floor or table.

How to Play:
Have students pair up, mix their sets of cards together, and play Memory with the combined set. They are to take turns turning over two cards to find word matches. When they find a match, they must correctly read the word to keep it. If they cannot correctly read the word, the match must be turned back over, and play passes back to the other player.

22 Synonym or Antonym Match

Objective: introduce and reinforce antonyms

Materials: Synonym cards (page 117) or Antonym cards (page 118), paper cutter, rubber bands

Getting Ready:
1. Reproduce a set of cards for each student.
2. Cut apart the cards and secure them with a rubber band.
3. Give each student a set of cards, and review the words together.

Setting: Two to four players work on a flat surface, such as a floor or table.

How to Play:
Have students pair up, mix two sets of cards together, and play Memory with the combined set. They are to take turns turning over two cards to find word matches. When they find a match, they must correctly read the words. If they cannot correctly read the words, the match must be turned back over, and play passes back to the other player.

Alternate Version: Instead of having students match two identical synonym or antonym pairs, students play with one set of cards which has the two synonyms or antonyms cut apart. Their goal is to match each word with its synonym or antonym (e.g., synonyms *small* and *little* or antonyms *easy* and *difficult*). Play as usual, but leave words faceup after turned over (otherwise it is a bit too hard). When counting up matches, players must say the two words in each pair.

Published by Frank Schaffer Publications.
Copyright protected.

0-7682-3412-3
101 Easy Reading Games

BINGO

Play the Bingo games in this section as you do any other Bingo games. You may want to laminate Bingo boards for repeated use, and use paper or plastic chips as the bingo markers.

23 Number BINGO

Objective: introduce and reinforce number words

Materials: Number Word cards (page 103); cardstock; BINGO game card (page 22); pencils; BINGO chips

Getting Ready:
1. Reproduce a BINGO game card for each student. Reproduce one set of word cards on cardstock, then cut them apart and secure the deck with a rubber band.
2. List the number words on the board or copy the list below onto an overhead transparency.
3. As a group, practice reading the words.
4. Have students randomly write the number words on their BINGO cards, using each word at least once.
5. Pass out BINGO chips to each student.

Setting: Students sit at desks or tables with a working surface.

How to Play:
1. Shuffle word cards and stack them in a pile, facedown.
2. Draw the card off the top and read it aloud.
3. Students find the word, if they have it, and point to that square on their BINGO cards. After everyone has pointed, show and spell the word. Students pointing to the correct word may then cover it with a BINGO chip.
4. Return the cards to the deck and continue until someone has BINGO—five horizontal, vertical, or diagonal squares covered.

Alternate Version: Have students write numerals, rather than number words, on their BINGO boards. Point to each word on the list as you draw it, and allow students to point to the corresponding numeral on their boards. After everyone has pointed, read the word aloud and write the numeral next to it. Students pointing to the correct numeral may then cover it with a BINGO chip. Play until someone gets BINGO.

zero	one	two	three
four	five	six	seven
eight	nine	ten	eleven
twelve	thirteen	fourteen	fifteen
sixteen	seventeen	eighteen	nineteen
twenty	thirty	forty	fifty
sixty	seventy	eighty	ninety

BINGO Game Card

B	I	N	G	O
		free		

BINGO

 **Animal BINGO**

Objective: introduce and reinforce animal words

Materials: BINGO game card (page 22), Animal Picture cards (pages 104–105), scissors, glue sticks, BINGO chips

Getting Ready:
1. Reproduce a set of Animal Picture cards and a BINGO game card for each student.
2. List the animal words on the board or copy the list below onto an overhead transparency. Take turns reading them.
3. Pass out Animal Picture cards, BINGO cards, and BINGO chips.
4. Students cut and paste 24 of the animals on a BINGO game card.
5. Pass out BINGO chips to each student.

Setting: Students sit at desks or tables with a working surface.

How to Play:
1. Randomly point to an animal word (don't say it) from your list on the board or overhead.
2. Students silently read the word and look for a picture of that animal on their cards. If they see it, they point to it with their fingers.
3. Once everyone who thinks they have the animal picture is pointing to it, read the animal word aloud. Students who were pointing to the correct animal may cover it with a BINGO chip.
4. Continue until someone has BINGO—five horizontal, vertical, or diagonal squares covered.

Alternate Version: Have students glue or write animal words, rather than pictures, on their bingo cards. You may reproduce and pass out the words below. Make one copy for yourself (or use Animal Word cards on pages 106–107) to cut apart and draw randomly out of a box. Read each word aloud as students find and cover it on their own cards.

alligator	buffalo	butterfly	centipede	cheetah	cobra
coyote	crab	dragonfly	dinosaur	donkey	eagle
eel	elephant	gecko	giraffe	gorilla	hamster
hippopotamus	horse	jellyfish	kangaroo	kitten	lizard
llama	monkey	moose	octopus	ostrich	platypus
pelican	penguin	quail	rabbit	rhinoceros	scorpion
sea horse	shark	slug	snake	snail	spider
squirrel	starfish	swine	turtle	whale	zebra

Published by Frank Schaffer Publications.
Copyright protected.

0-7682-3412-3
101 Easy Reading Games

BINGO

25 Food BINGO

Objective: introduce and reinforce 40 food words—bananas, bread, broccoli, cabbage, cake, candy, carrot, cheese, cherries, croissant, drumstick, eggs, eggplant, green beans, French fries, grapes, hamburger, ice cream bar, lima bean, milk, muffin, mushroom, pasta, peas, peanuts, pepper, pie, pineapple, pizza, popcorn, potato, pumpkin, sandwich, shrimp, soda, steak, strawberry, tea, tomato, zucchini

Materials: BINGO game card (page 22), Food Picture cards (pages 108–109), scissors, glue sticks, BINGO chips

Getting Ready:
1. Reproduce a set of Food Picture cards and a BINGO game card for each student.
2. List the food words on the board or copy the list below onto an overhead transparency. Take turns reading them.
3. Pass out Food Picture cards, BINGO cards, and BINGO chips.
4. Students cut and paste 24 of the foods on a BINGO game card.

Setting: Students sit at desks or tables with a working surface.

How to Play:
1. Randomly point to a food word (don't say it) from your list on the board or overhead.
2. Students silently read the word and look for a picture of that food on their cards. If they see it, they point to it with their fingers.
3. Once everyone who thinks they have the food picture is pointing to it, read the food word aloud. Students who were pointing to the correct food may cover it with a BINGO chip.
4. Continue until someone has BINGO—five horizontal, vertical, or diagonal squares covered.

Alternate Version: Have students glue or write food words, rather than pictures, on their bingo cards. You may reproduce and pass out the words below. Make one copy for yourself (or use Food Word cards on pages 110–111) to cut apart and draw randomly out of a box. Read each word aloud as students find and cover it on their own cards.

bananas	bread	broccoli	cabbage	cake
candy	carrot	cheese	cherries	croissant
drumstick	eggs	eggplant	green beans	French fries
grapes	hamburger	ice cream bar	lima bean	milk
muffin	mushroom	pasta	peas	peanuts
pepper	pie	pineapple	pizza	popcorn
potato	pumpkin	sandwich	shrimp	soda
steak	strawberry	tea	tomato	zucchini

Published by Frank Schaffer Publications.
Copyright protected.

0-7682-3412-3
101 Easy Reading Games

BINGO

 **Sight Word BINGO**

Objective: introduce and reinforce sight words

Materials: BINGO game card (page 22), BINGO chips

Getting Ready:

1. Reproduce a BINGO game card for each student.
2. Select and print some words from the word list (see below) on the board, or copy the list onto a transparency and put it on the overhead projector. As a group, read some or all of the words in the list.

Setting: Students work at desks or a table where there is a work surface.

How to Play:

1. Students print a different word in each square on their card.
2. Randomly name words on the list, or cut up a copy of the list and randomly draw.
3. If a student has that word, he covers it.
4. As you play, keep track of words called.
5. The first one who has covered five words horizontally, vertically, or diagonally shouts "BINGO!"

Sight Word List

about	afterward	against	always	anyone	around
because	been	before	best	better	both
bring	caller	came	carry	clean	cold
come	could	does	done	down	draw
drinking	everyone	falling	faster	finding	first
found	four	from	full	funny	gave
give	goes	going	good	grow	have
help	here	him	holding	hurt	into
its	jumping	just	keep	kind	knew
knight	laugh	light	little	long	look
made	make	many	much	must	myself
never	new	nothing	now	off	older
once	only	open	ourselves	out	over
own	player	please	pick	pretty	pulling
putting	read	right	round	said	seesaw
saying	seven	shall	she	show	sing
sleep	small	some	soon	start	student
take	teacher	thank	that	the	their
them	then	there	these	they	think
this	today	together	tomorrow	try	under
upon	use	very	walk	want	warm
was	wash	well	went	were	what
when	where	willing	wish	with	worker
would	writer	yes	you	your	zoo

BINGO

 **Synonym or Antonym BINGO**

Objective: introduce and reinforce antonym pairs

Materials: Synonym cards (page 117) or Antonym cards (page 118); cardstock; BINGO game card (page 22); pencils; BINGO chips

Getting Ready:

1. Reproduce a BINGO game card for each student. Reproduce one set of synonym or antonym word cards on cardstock, then cut them apart and secure the deck with a rubber band.*
2. List the synonym or antonym pairs on the board or copy the list onto an overhead transparency.
3. As a group, practice reading the word pairs.
4. Have students randomly write the words on their BINGO cards, using one word per box.
5. Pass out BINGO chips to each student.

Setting: Students sit at desks or tables with a working surface.

How to Play:

1. Shuffle the cards and stack them in a pile, facedown.
2. One at a time, choose a card, list one of the words on the board, and read it aloud.
3. Students think of the synonym or antonym to that word, find it in any column on their cards, and point to it with their fingers.
4. Once everyone who thinks they have the word is pointing to it, reveal the correct answer and write it on the board next to the original word. Students who were pointing correctly may cover the word with a BINGO chip.
5. Continue until someone has BINGO—five horizontal, vertical, or diagonal squares covered.

*You may, instead, choose to write words on large index cards. Write one word on one side of the card and its synonym or antonym on the back of the card. Later, during play, choose one card at a time and hold it up for students to read one side. Flip the card over to reveal the correct synonym or antonym after students have indicated their choices on their boards.

Published by Frank Schaffer Publications.
Copyright protected.

0-7682-3412-3
101 Easy Reading Games

BINGO

 **Consonant Blend Bingo**

Objective: introduce and reinforce words with initial and final consonant blends

Materials: sturdy cardstock; paper cutter; any five types of word cards (see list below); BINGO game card (page 22); pencils; BINGO chips

Word Cards for Use with Consonant Blend Bingo
"GR" Cards (93)
"TR" Cards (94)
"CR" Cards (95)
"PL" Cards (96)
"SL" Cards (97)
"SM" and "SN" Cards (98)
"SK," "SP," "SQ," "ST," and "SW" Cards (99–100)
"NG" Cards (101)

Getting Ready:
1. Reproduce a BINGO game card for each student.*
2. Choose the five word lists you are going to use and print them on the board or on an overhead transparency. As a group, read the words in each list.

Setting: Students work at desks or a table where there is a work surface.

How to Play:
1. Students write one blend type (e.g., "GR") in each box across the top of the card. They then choose and print words in each square on their card.
2. Randomly name words from your lists, or cut up copies and randomly draw.
3. Students use a BINGO chip to cover each word they hear.
4. The first one who has covered five words in a row, horizontally, vertically, or diagonally shouts "BINGO!"

*Cover up the BINGO letters before copying the cards so the top of each column is a blank box.

Quiz Challenge

The Quiz Challenge games in this section may remind you of the game Jeopardy. You set up each Quiz Challenge in a similar way, with a grid of questions that are worth various point values. If you plan to play this game often, you may want to prepare a permanent Quiz Challenge board for yourself in one of the following ways.

- Construct a board out of foam board and library pockets. Write "Quiz Challenge" at the top, and attach a grid of pockets that is five across and six down. This will allow you to place the category titles at the top of each column of five questions. Label the library pockets with point values according to the pattern on page 29. You will be able to slip the cards into the pockets before each game and easily pull them out as you play.

- Purchase and set aside a cork board with push pins. Before play, write a point value on the back of each card and attach it to the board with the push pins.

- Purchase and set aside a pocket chart that has room for five columns and six rows. Make rectangular cards from construction paper that are big enough to cover the question cards, and label them with point values according to the pattern on page 29. This is a very convenient way to set up your board, because cards slide easily in and out of the pockets and column headings can be seen through the clear plastic.

You may choose to select a few players for each round, break the students into teams with one spokesperson for each team, or break into small groups of four: three players and one moderator to read the cards.

Each card that has been created for this section has a category title on the top of it, as well as a point value. You may award that exact number of points, or award points in multiples of the given number (i.e., 10 or 100 for a 1 point card) for a correct answer. Keep track of points on the board or assign the job of scorekeeper to one student. He may keep track by writing the name of the person who won each question in the corresponding space on the score sheet (page 29) and adding totals at the end. Teams or individuals may compete against each other, or students may compete as a class to hit a designated target or "beat the teacher."

To add fun and excitement, create a few special bonus cards to slip in with some of the questions. Bonus ideas include "double points," "triple points," "5 extra minutes of recess," "10 minutes of computer time," and so on.

Before play, designate a way for students to "buzz in" when they know the answer. You may have students raise hands, touch their noses, slap the table, ring a bell, use an electronic device, or make up your own method. Just be sure to be clear with students which method you are using and do your best to fairly determine who rings in first.

Card categories from different Quiz Challenge game sets may be used interchangeably as desired without affecting the game at all. Feel free to add more questions to each category as you desire, and have fun increasing reading skills as you play!

Quiz Challenge Score Sheet

1	1	1	1	1
2	2	2	2	2
3	3	3	3	3
4	4	4	4	4
5	5	5	5	5

Published by Frank Schaffer Publications.

0-7682-3412-3
101 Easy Reading Games

Quiz Challenge

29 Vocabulary Quiz Challenge

Objective: expand and develop vocabulary with compound words, contractions, synonyms, antonyms, and plural words

Materials: Quiz Challenge board (see introduction), Vocabulary Quiz Challenge cards (page 120), optional Quiz Challenge score sheet (page 29), cardstock, paper cutter

Getting Ready:

1. Reproduce one set of Vocabulary Quiz Challenge cards and cut them apart. Place them in the appropriate places on your Quiz Challenge board.
2. If desired, make a copy of the Quiz Challenge score sheet on paper or an overhead transparency. Write the category titles across the top.
3. Determine and communicate rules of play to the class (i.e., number of players, groups or individuals, scorekeeping, and method of "buzzing in").

Setting: Players stand or sit somewhere they can see questions and "buzz in."

How to Play:

1. The first player chooses a category and a point value (e.g., Antonyms for 3 points).
2. Read the question.
3. Call on the first player who "buzzes in."
4. The player states his answer. If correct, he is awarded the amount of points on the card. If incorrect, another player may buzz in. If no students can answer correctly, read the correct answer and "X" out that space on the score sheet.
5. Continue play according to the Quiz Challenge rules until each question has been used or you are out of time.
6. Add the points to see who won.

Published by Frank Schaffer Publications.
Copyright protected.

0-7682-3412-3
101 Easy Reading Games

Quiz Challenge

 **Homophone Quiz Challenge**

Objective: expand and develop vocabulary with homophones

Materials: Quiz Challenge board (see introduction), Homophone Quiz Challenge cards (page 121), optional Quiz Challenge score sheet (page 29), cardstock, paper cutter

Getting Ready:
1. Reproduce one set of Homophone Quiz Challenge cards and cut them apart. Place them in the appropriate places on your Quiz Challenge board.
2. If desired, make a copy of the Quiz Challenge score sheet on paper or an overhead transparency. Write the category titles across the top.
3. Determine and communicate rules of play to the class (i.e., number of players, groups or individuals, scorekeeping, and method of "buzzing in").

Setting: Players stand or sit somewhere they can see questions and "buzz in."

How to Play:
1. The first player chooses a category and a point value (e.g., Write It for 1 point).
2. Read the question.
3. Call on the first player who "buzzes in."
4. The player states her answer. If correct, she is awarded the amount of points on the card. If incorrect, another player may buzz in. If no students can answer correctly, read the correct answer and "X" out that space on the score sheet.
5. Continue play according to the Quiz Challenge rules until each question has been used or you are out of time.
6. Add the points to see who won.

Quiz Challenge

31 Comprehension Quiz Challenge

Objective: expand and develop comprehension skills

Materials: Quiz Challenge board (see introduction), Comprehension Quiz Challenge cards (page 127), optional Quiz Challenge score sheet (page 29), cardstock, paper cutter

Getting Ready:

1. Reproduce one set of Comprehension Quiz Challenge cards and cut them apart. Place them in the appropriate places on your Quiz Challenge board.
2. If desired, make a copy of the Quiz Challenge score sheet on paper or an overhead transparency. Write the category titles across the top.
3. Determine and communicate rules of play to the class (i.e., number of players, groups or individuals, scorekeeping, and method of "buzzing in").

Setting: Players stand or sit somewhere they can see questions and "buzz in."

How to Play:

1. The first player chooses a category and a point value (e.g., Cause & Effect for 4 points).
2. Read the question.
3. Call on the first player who "buzzes in."
4. The player states his answer. If correct, he is awarded the amount of points on the card. If incorrect, another player may buzz in. If no students can answer correctly, read the correct answer and "X" out that space on the score sheet.
5. Continue play according to the Quiz Challenge rules until each question has been used or you are out of time.
6. Add the points to see who won.

Published by Frank Schaffer Publications.
Copyright protected.

0-7682-3412-3
101 Easy Reading Games

Quiz Challenge

 **Story Elements Quiz Challenge**

Objective: demonstrate comprehension of a specified story by identifying story elements

Materials: Quiz Challenge board (see introduction), Story Elements Quiz Challenge cards (page 122), optional Quiz Challenge score sheet (page 29), cardstock, paper cutter

Getting Ready:
1. Reproduce one set of Story Elements Quiz Challenge cards and cut them apart. Place them in the appropriate places on your Quiz Challenge board.
2. If desired, make a copy of the Quiz Challenge score sheet on paper or an overhead transparency. Write the category titles across the top.
3. Determine and communicate rules of play to the class (i.e., number of players, groups or individuals, scorekeeping, and method of "buzzing in").

Setting: Players stand or sit somewhere they can see questions and "buzz in."

How to Play:
1. Use this game to review a book or story everyone has read. Answers are not given on the cards, so the moderator must determine what the correct answers are for each question.
2. The first player chooses a category and a point value (e.g., Character for 5 points).
3. Read the question.
4. Call on the first player who "buzzes in."
5. The player states his answer. If correct, he is awarded the amount of points on the card. If incorrect, another player may buzz in. If no students can answer correctly, read the correct answer and "X" out that space on the score sheet.
6. Continue play according to the Quiz Challenge rules until each question has been used or you are out of time.
7. Add the points to see who won.

Alternate Version:
Prepare a set of Fairy Tale cards (page 123). When placing the Quiz Challenge questions in the appropriate places on your Quiz Challenge board, also insert one Fairy Tale card for each question. When it is time to read the question, begin by identifying the story (e.g., for Setting for 1 point with the Cinderella card, say, "Think of the fairy tale Cinderella. Where does this story take place?"). Continue play as usual.

For a simpler version, select one fairy tale for each category or for the whole board. Play as usual.

Quiz Challenge

 Fairy Tale Quiz Challenge

Objective: demonstrate comprehension of story elements for a variety of fairy tales

Materials: Quiz Challenge board (see introduction), Fairy Tale Quiz Challenge cards (page 124), optional Quiz Challenge score sheet (page 29), cardstock, paper cutter

Getting Ready:

1. Reproduce one set of Fairy Tale Quiz Challenge cards and cut them apart. Place them in the appropriate places on your Quiz Challenge board.
2. If desired, make a copy of the Quiz Challenge score sheet on paper or an overhead transparency. Write the category titles across the top.
3. Determine and communicate rules of play to the class (i.e., number of players, groups or individuals, scorekeeping, and method of "buzzing in").

Setting: Players stand or sit somewhere they can see questions and "buzz in."

How to Play:

1. The first player chooses a category and a point value (e.g., Lesson Learned for 4 points).
2. Read the question.
3. Call on the first player who "buzzes in."
4. The player states his answer. If correct, he is awarded the amount of points on the card. If incorrect, another player may buzz in. If no students can answer correctly, read the correct answer and "X" out that space on the score board.
5. Continue play according to the Quiz Challenge rules until each question has been used or you are out of time.
6. Add the points to see who won.

 **Combination Quiz Challenge**

How to Play:
Play according to regular Quiz Challenge rules. Combine different sets of Quiz Challenge cards or write your own. Use this format as a fun way to review materials you have covered or to preview new material.

Quick Draw

The purpose of Quick Draw is to develop and demonstrate vocabulary and comprehension skills. Students will deepen their understanding of words, concepts, and story elements as they are challenged to show what they visualize when reading. These games also are a great way to address different learning styles and allow students with visual and artistic skills to shine!

The Quick Draw games in this section all follow a simple format—one player sketches a designated word while others shout out guesses. This may be played as a whole class, as teams, or with partners.

In the whole-class version, one artist at a time draws a word as class members earn points to hit a target number.

The team version still involves the whole class in group play, but teams take turns drawing. The team whose turn it is has a time limit for each word. If they are unable to guess correctly in the time allowed, the other team has a chance to "steal" the point by correctly guessing the word. Play alternates between the two teams. Teams earn points to compete with each other and the team with the most points at the end is the winner.

For partner play, students pair up. Each pair has one set of cards to draw from. Players take turns drawing and guessing.

However you choose to play, Quick Draw is a great way to practice vocabulary and comprehension!

Published by Frank Schaffer Publications.
Copyright protected.

0-7682-3412-3
101 Easy Reading Games

Quick Draw

 Animal or Food Quick Draw

Objective: reinforce understanding of vocabulary words, practice categorization skills

Materials: Animal Word cards (pages 106–107) and/or Food Word cards (pages 110–111), scissors, paper bag

Getting Ready:
1. Reproduce either or both sets of the word cards.
2. Cut apart the cards and fold each one.
3. Place them in a paper bag.

Setting: Students gather at the board.

How to Play:
1. Players take turns drawing a word from the bag and drawing a picture on the board that represents the word.
2. Others shout out their guesses.
3. The first person to shout out the correct word must then identify the category it came from (animal or food). If he does name the correct category, it is his turn to draw. If not, continue calling on players until someone correctly names the category.
4. Continue taking turns drawing until all cards have been used.

Alternate Version: Make your own cards for several different categories and play the same way as above. This will reinforce categorizing skills. If your class has studied animal classification (bird, fish, mammal, reptile, amphibian), you may also have students classify by these types.

 Sight Word Quick Draw

Objective: reinforce understanding of vocabulary sight words

Materials: Sight Word cards (pages 112–115), scissors, paper bag

Getting Ready:
1. Reproduce the word cards. Remove any words you feel would be too complicated for students to draw (e.g., does, must, was, were, and so on).
2. Cut apart the cards and fold each one.
3. Place them in a paper bag.

Setting: Students gather at the board.

How to Play:
1. Players take turns drawing a word from the bag and drawing a picture on the board that represents the word.
2. Others shout out their guesses.
3. The first person to shout out the correct word must then spell it correctly. If he does spell it correctly, it is his turn to draw. If not, continue calling on players until someone correctly spells the word.
4. Continue taking turns drawing until all cards have been used or you run out of time.

Published by Frank Schaffer Publications.
Copyright protected.

0-7682-3412-3
101 Easy Reading Games

Quick Draw

 **Compound Word Quick Draw**

Objective: reinforce understanding of compound words

Materials: Compound Word cards (page 119), scissors, paper bag

Getting Ready:
1. Reproduce the word cards.
2. Cut apart the cards and fold each one.
3. Place them in a paper bag.

Setting: Students gather at the board.

How to Play:
1. Players take turns drawing a compound word from the bag and drawing a picture on the board that represents the word. This may be one picture that represents the whole word or two pictures that represent each smaller word (e.g., *swordfish* could either be drawn as a swordfish, or as a sword and a fish).
2. Others shout out their guesses.
3. The first person to shout out the correct word must then identify the two smaller words that make up the compound word. If she does correctly identify them, it is her turn to draw. If not, continue calling on players until someone correctly names the two smaller words.
4. Continue taking turns drawing until all cards have been used or you are out of time.

 Homophone Quick Draw

Objective: reinforce understanding of homophones

Materials: Homophone cards (page 116), scissors, paper bag

Getting Ready:
1. Reproduce the word cards.
2. Cut apart the cards and fold each one.
3. Place them in a paper bag.

Setting: Students gather at the board.

How to Play:
1. Players take turns drawing a homophone from the bag and drawing a picture on the board that represents the word.
2. Others shout out their guesses.
3. The first person to shout out the correct word must then give the definition and spell it correctly. If he does both correctly, it is his turn to draw. If not, continue calling on players until someone answers correctly.
4. Continue taking turns drawing until all cards have been used or you are out of time.

Alternate Version: In addition to spelling and defining the word once it is guessed, you may have the player who is guessing state the homophone's pair and definition (e.g., for *one*, the player would also have to name and define *won*).

Published by Frank Schaffer Publications.
Copyright protected.

0-7682-3412-3
101 Easy Reading Games

Quick Draw

 **Synonym Quick Draw**

Objective: reinforce understanding of synonyms

Materials: Synonym cards (page 117), scissors, paper bag

Getting Ready:
1. Reproduce the word cards.
2. Cut apart the cards and fold each one.
3. Place them in a paper bag.

Setting: Students gather at the board.

How to Play:
1. Players take turns drawing a synonym card from the bag and drawing a picture on the board that represents one of the words.
2. Others shout out their guesses.
3. The first person to shout out the correct answer must then name the correct synonym of the drawn word. If he names it correctly, it is his turn to draw. If not, continue calling on players until someone answers correctly.
4. Continue taking turns drawing until all cards have been used or you are out of time

 **Antonym Quick Draw**

Objective: reinforce understanding of antonyms

Materials: Antonym cards (page 118), scissors, paper bag

Getting Ready:
1. Reproduce the word cards.
2. Cut apart the cards and fold each one.
3. Place them in a paper bag.

Setting: Students gather at the board.

How to Play:
1. Players take turns drawing an antonym card from the bag and drawing a picture on the board that represents one of the words.
2. Others shout out their guesses.
3. The first person to shout out the correct answer must then name the correct antonym of the drawn word. If he names it correctly, it is his turn to draw. If not, continue calling on players until someone answers correctly.
4. Continue taking turns drawing until all cards have been used or you are out of time.

Published by Frank Schaffer Publications.
Copyright protected.

0-7682-3412-3
101 Easy Reading Games

Quick Draw

 **Story Element Quick Draw**

Objective: introduce and reinforce story elements using well-known children's stories

Materials: Fairy Tale cards (page 123) scissors, paper bag, two-minute timer

Getting Ready:
1. Reproduce the cards.
2. Cut apart the cards and place them in a paper bag.
3. Divide students into two teams.

Setting: Students gather at the board.

How to Play:
1. Establish which story element you will be focusing on in your game (characters, setting, problem, solution, or events). Here are three ways to decide:
   - Focus on one story element for the whole game.
   - Play in rounds, with each round dedicated to a different story element.
   - With each draw, use a die or spinner marked with the story elements to determine the category.
2. Students take turns drawing a card from the bag.
3. A player has two minutes to draw a picture on the board to convey the designated story element of that story.
4. Students take turns shouting out guesses when their team is drawing.
5. When a team guesses correctly within the time limit, they get a point and another turn. If the team does not guess correctly, the other team has a chance to guess and "steal" the point. It is then the other team's turn to draw.

Alternate Version: Instead of playing with fairy tales, play with a story or stories you have read together as a class.

 **Comprehension Skills Quick Draw**

Objective: reinforce understanding of classifying and drawing conclusions

Materials: Classify: Name This Group cards or Riddles (Conclusions) cards (page 127), scissors, paper bag

Getting Ready:
1. Reproduce the word cards. You may choose to write more of your own cards.
2. Cut apart the cards and fold each one.
3. Place them in a paper bag.

Setting: Students gather at the board.

How to Play:
1. Players take turns drawing a card from the bag and drawing a picture on the board that represents the word in parentheses. Before drawing, the player reads the clue.
2. Other players shout out their guesses.
3. The first person to shout out the correct word gets to draw next.
4. Continue taking turns drawing until all cards have been used or you are out of time.

Published by Frank Schaffer Publications.
Copyright protected.

0-7682-3412-3
101 Easy Reading Games

Board Games

The board games in this section follow the general pattern of board games involving a game board with a start and an end, game markers for each player, and cards with questions on them. You may choose to use the game board provided in this section, make up your own, or use game boards you have from other games. The cards and instructions will work with any of these type of simple game boards and any game markers. To make the game board on pages 42–43, match the two sides at the dotted lines and tape together.

 ## Blend or Sight Word Board Game

Objective: demonstrate fluency with sight words and words that begin with blends

Materials: game board pattern (pages 42–43), sturdy cardstock, rubber bands, game markers, any type of word cards (pages 89–101 or pages 112–115, see list below)

Word Cards for Use with Decoding Memory
"BR" Cards (89–90)
"FR" Cards (91–92)
"GR" Cards (93)
"TR" Cards (94)
"CR" Cards (95)
"PL" Cards (96)
"SL" Cards (97)
"SM" and "SN" Cards (98)
"SK," "SP," "SQ," "ST," and "SW" Cards (99–100)
"NG" Cards (101)
Sight Word Cards (112–115)

Getting Ready:
1. For each set of three to four players, reproduce a game board and the chosen set of word cards on sturdy cardstock.
2. Trim and glue a game board to the inside of a file folder. Decorate with markers, stickers, and so on.
3. Cut apart the cards. On the back of each card, assign and write a point value in a circle on the top right corner. Stack and secure the cards with a rubber band.

Setting: Two to four players sit at a table around the game board.

How to Play:
1. Pass out materials to groups. To begin, one player shuffles the cards and places them word-side up on the game board.
2. Players place their markers in the "start" space.
3. The first player looks at the card before picking it up and reads the word.
4. If the other players agree that he read it correctly, he can move the number of spaces shown on the back of the card. If incorrect, he moves no spaces. He then returns the card to the bottom of the deck or places it in a discard pile.
5. The first player to reach the "end" is declared the winner.

Published by Frank Schaffer Publications.
Copyright protected.

0-7682-3412-3
101 Easy Reading Games

Board Games

 **Blend Word Family Board Game**

Objective: introduce and reinforce several blends and word families

Materials: game board pattern (pages 42–43), Blend Word Family cards (page 102), Blend List (see below), sturdy cardstock, rubber bands, game markers

Getting Ready:
1. For each set of three to four players, reproduce a game board, a Blend List, and Blend Word Family cards on sturdy cardstock.
2. Trim and glue a game board to the inside of a file folder. Decorate with markers, stickers, and so on.
3. Cut apart the cards and secure the deck with a rubber band.
4. Explain that the words listed on the cards are suggestions. There may be other words that begin with a blend and are part of the given word family. Any questions regarding an answer can be directed to you.

Setting: Two to four players sit at a table around the game board.

How to Play:
1. Pass out materials to groups. Explain that the Blend List is to help players remember some basic blends. To begin, one player shuffles the cards and places them facedown on the game board.
2. Players place their markers in the "start" space.
3. The first player draws a card and passes it facedown to the player on his right.
4. That person reads the word family at the top of the card (e.g., "-ace").
5. The player must say as many words as he can think of that begin with a blend and end with the given word family. If he is correct, he moves ahead the number of words he names. If he cannot name any, he does not move at all.
6. Place the card facedown on the bottom of the deck or in a discard pile.
7. The first player to reach the "end" is declared the winner.

Blend List

bl, cl, fl, gl, pl, sl

br, cr, dr, fr, gr, pr, tr

sm, sn, st, sw, sk, sp

Published by Frank Schaffer Publications.
Copyright protected.

0-7682-3412-3
101 Easy Reading Games

Board Games

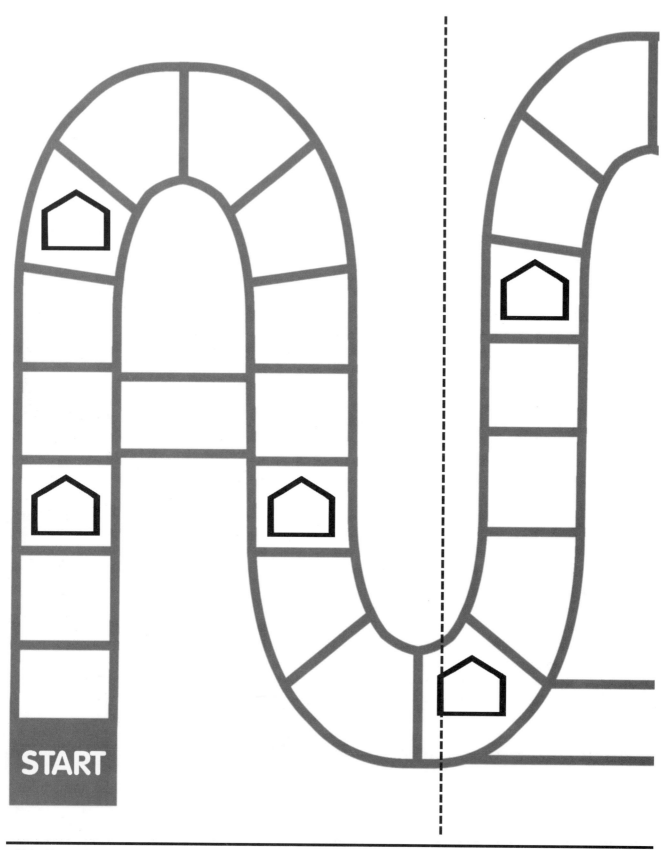

START

0-7682-3412-3
101 Easy Reading Games

Board Games

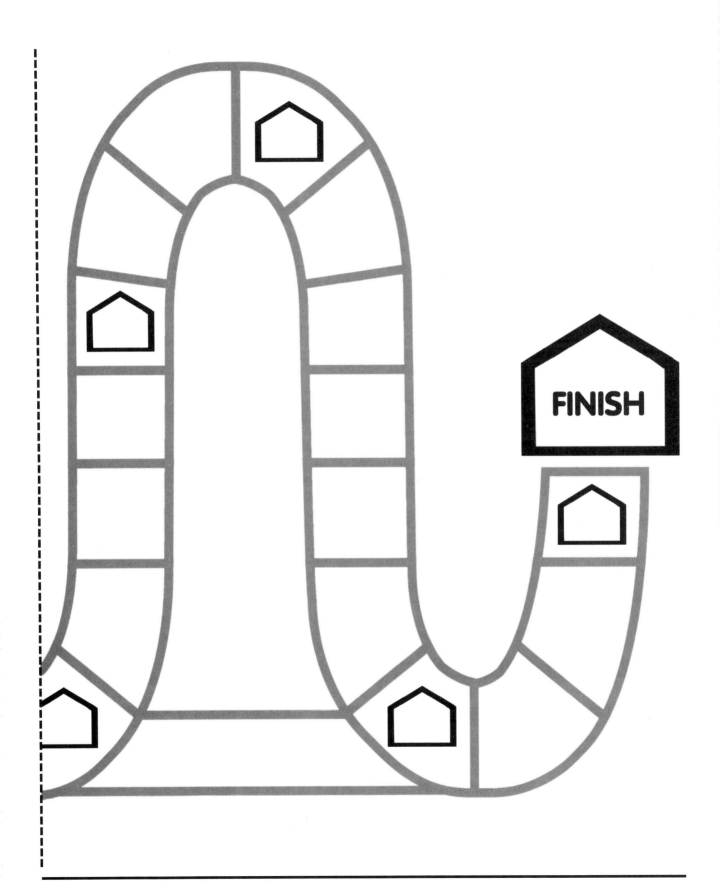

0-7682-3412-3
101 Easy Reading Games

Board Games

Number Word Board Game

Objective: demonstrate knowledge of and fluency with number words

Materials: game board pattern (pages 42–43), Number Word cards (page 103), sturdy cardstock, rubber bands, game markers

Getting Ready:
1. For each set of three to four players, reproduce a game board and Number Word cards on sturdy cardstock.
2. Trim and glue a game board to the inside of a file folder. Decorate with markers, stickers, and so on.
3. Cut apart the cards. On the back of each Number Word card, write the numeral that corresponds with the number word on the front. Assign a point value and write it in a circle on the top right corner. Stack and secure the cards with a rubber band.

Setting: Two to four players sit at a table around the game board.

How to Play:
1. Pass out materials to groups. To begin, one player shuffles the cards and places them word-side up on the game board.
2. Players place their markers in the "start" space.
3. The first player looks at the card before picking it up and reads the word aloud.
4. She can then pick up the card, flip it over, and look on the back to check her answer. If correct, she can move the number of spaces shown on the card. If incorrect, she moves no spaces. She then returns the card to the bottom of the deck or places it in a discard pile.
5. The first player to reach the "end" is declared the winner.

Animal Word or Food Word Board Games

Objective: demonstrate knowledge of and fluency with animal words

How to Play:
Set up and play as the Color and Number Word Board Game above, but use Animal Word and Picture cards (pages 104–107) or Food Word and Picture cards (pages 108–111) in place of Number Word cards. Cut out both picture and word cards, and glue the correct words to the backs of the pictures. (As an alternative, you may just reproduce the picture cards and write the correct words on the backs.) Add the point value in a circle on the top right of the picture side of each card. To play, players place cards word-side up on the board, read each word, and turn to the picture side to check each answer.

Published by Frank Schaffer Publications.
Copyright protected.

0-7682-3412-3
101 Easy Reading Games

Board Games

 **Synonym or Antonym Board Game**

Objective: demonstrate knowledge of synonyms and antonyms

Materials: game board pattern (pages 42–43), Synonym or Antonym cards (pages 117–118), sturdy cardstock, rubber bands, game markers

Getting Ready:

1. For each set of three to four players, reproduce a game board and two sets of Synonym and Antonym cards on sturdy cardstock. (You may want to use different colors of cardstock for the two different sets. This will help keep the synonym and antonym cards separate.)
2. Trim and glue a game board to the inside of a file folder. Decorate with markers, stickers, and so on.
3. Cut apart the cards. Assign a point value and write it in a circle on the top right corner of each card. Stack and secure each set of cards with a rubber band.

Setting: Two to four players sit at a table around the game board.

How to Play:

1. Pass out materials to groups. Only pass out one set of cards, synonyms or antonyms, and inform players which set they are using. To begin, one player shuffles the cards and places them facedown on the game board.
2. Players place their markers in the "start" space.
3. The first player draws a card and passes it facedown to the player on his right.
4. That person reads one of the words on the card (e.g., "small").
5. The player must state the antonym or synonym of the given word. If correct, he can move the number of spaces shown on the card. If incorrect, he moves no spaces. He then returns the card to the bottom of the deck or places it in a discard pile.
6. The first player to reach the "end" is declared the winner.

Published by Frank Schaffer Publications.
Copyright protected.

0-7682-3412-3
101 Easy Reading Games

Board Games

Objective: reinforce various skills

Materials: game board pattern (pages 42–43), any set of Quiz Challenge cards, sturdy cardstock, rubber bands, game markers

Getting Ready:

1. For each set of three to four players, reproduce a game board and a set of cards on sturdy cardstock.
2. Trim and glue a game board to the inside of a file folder. Decorate with markers, stickers, and so on.
3. Cut apart the cards. On the back of each card, write the correct answer. Assign a point value (use same value designated on front of card). Write it in a circle on the top right corner. Cross the answer off the front of each card with heavy black marker. Stack and secure the cards with a rubber band.

Setting: Two to four players sit at a table around the game board.

How to Play:

1. Pass out materials to groups. To begin, one player shuffles the cards and places them question-side up on the game board.
2. Players place their markers in the "start" space.
3. The first player looks at the card before picking it up and names the correct answer.
4. She can then pick up the card, flip it over, and look on the back to check her answer. If correct, she can move the number of spaces shown on the card. If incorrect, she moves no spaces. She then returns the card to the bottom of the deck or places it in a discard pile.
5. The first player to reach the "end" is declared the winner.

Card Games

This section contains games designed to play just as the timeless classics Go Fish, War, and Rummy. You may choose to play other card games, such as Old Maid, as well. The cards lend themselves well to many more games than there is room to list!

 **Consonant Blend Go Fish**

Objective: introduce and reinforce consonant blends

Materials: sturdy cardstock, paper cutter, any type of consonant blend cards (pages 89–101, see list below)

Word Cards for Use with Decoding Memory
"BR" Cards (89–90)
"FR" Cards (91–92)
"GR" Cards (93)
"TR" Cards (94)
"CR" Cards (95)
"PL" Cards (96)
"SL" Cards (97)
"SM" and "SN" Cards (98)
"SK," "SP," "SQ," "ST," and "SW" Cards (99–100)
"NG" Cards (101)

Getting Ready:
1. For each group of players, reproduce two sets of cards on sturdy cardstock.
2. Cut apart the cards and combine the decks. Secure each set with a rubber band.

Setting: Two to three players play at a table or on the floor.

How to Play:
1. Shuffle the cards and spread them out facedown in a "pond."
2. Allow each player to choose seven cards from the "pond."
3. Players look for word matches and lay them down, faceup, in front of them.
4. Players take turns asking "Do you have (word)?" in order to try for matches. If the other player has the card, he passes it over. If the other player does not have the card, he says, "Go fish," and the first player draws a card from the "pond."
5. After all the matches have been made, players count cards. To keep their cards, they must read each word before counting. If a player cannot read a word, he does not get to count that pair of cards.
6. The player with the most cards is declared the winner.

Alternate Version: Play as above, but mix together different consonant blends. Instead of asking for an exact word match, players ask, "Do you have a word with a (whichever type of) blend?" to try for matches. Players match cards with the same type of blend.

Card Games

 **Fluency Go Fish**

Objective: develop fluency with common words and sight words

Materials: sturdy cardstock, paper cutter, glue stick, any type of word cards (pages 103–115, see list below)

> **Word Cards for Use with Fluency Go Fish**
> Number Word cards (103)
> Animal Word cards (106–107)
> Food Word cards (110–111)
> Sight Word cards (112–115)

Getting Ready:

1. Reproduce two sets of cards on sturdy cardstock.
2. Cut apart the cards and combine the decks. If there are many of these cards, you may split them up into different sets. Secure each set with a rubber band.

Setting: Two to three players play at a table or on the floor.

How to Play:

1. Shuffle the cards and spread them out facedown in a "pond."
2. Allow each player to choose seven cards from the "pond."
3. Players look for word matches and lay them down, faceup, in front of them.
4. Players take turns asking, "Do you have (word)?" in order to try for matches. If the other player has the card, he passes it over. If the other player does not have the card, he says, "Go fish," and the first player draws a card from the "pond."
5. After all the matches have been made, players count cards. To keep their cards, they must read each word before counting. If a player cannot read a word, he does not get to count that pair of cards.
6. The player with the most cards is declared the winner.

Alternate Version: For Animal Word cards (106–107) and Food Word cards (110–111), you may copy and play for matches with Animal Picture and Food Picture cards. Play as above, but copy only one set of words and one set of pictures. Players match word cards with corresponding picture cards.

Published by Frank Schaffer Publications.
Copyright protected.

0-7682-3412-3
101 Easy Reading Games

Card Games

Homophone Go Fish

Objective: practice recognizing, matching, and defining homophones

Materials: Homophone cards (page 116), sturdy cardstock, paper cutter

Getting Ready:
1. Reproduce one set of cards on sturdy cardstock.
2. Cut apart the cards and secure them with a rubber band.

Setting: Two to three players play at a table or on the floor.

How to Play:
1. Shuffle the cards and spread them out facedown in a "pond."
2. Allow each player to choose seven cards from the "pond."
3. Players look for homophone pairs (e.g., *our* and *hour*), and lay them down.

4. Players take turns asking "Do you have (word)?" in order to find the homophone to a card from their hand. If the other player has the card, he passes it over. If the other player does not have the card, he says, "Go fish," and the first player draws a card from the "pond."
5. After all the matches have been made, players count cards. To keep their cards, they must read each word before counting. If a player cannot read a word, she does not get to count that pair of cards.
6. The player with the most cards is declared the winner.

Alternate Version: Play as above, but copy two sets of Homophone cards. Players ask for an exact word match. They ask "Do you have the word (homophone) that means (definition)?" Players make exact word matches. To keep the matches, players must correctly read each word and definition before counting cards.

Antonym or Synonym Go Fish

Objective: practice reading and matching corresponding antonyms or synonyms

Materials: Synonym or Antonym cards (pages 117 and 118), sturdy cardstock, paper cutter

Getting Ready:
1. Reproduce one set of cards on sturdy cardstock.
2. Cut apart the cards (also cut matching antonyms or synonyms apart on horizontal line) and secure them with a rubber band.

Setting: Two to three players play at a table or on the floor.

How to Play: Begin playing the same way as Homophone Go Fish. Players look for antonym or synonym pairs (e.g., *give* and *take*), and lay them down. Players take turns asking "Do you have the antonym (or synonym) of (word)?" If the other player has the card, he passes it over. If not, he says, "Go fish," and the first player draws a card. After all the matches have been made, players read each word as they count cards. The player with the most cards wins.

Card Games

 War with Words

Objective: practice word fluency and alphabetical order

Materials: sturdy cardstock, paper cutter, rubber bands, any type of word cards (pages 89–115, see list below)

Word Cards for Use with War with Words
Blend Word cards (89–101)
Number Word cards (103)
Animal Word cards (106–107)
Food Word cards (110–111)
Sight Word cards (112–115)

Getting Ready:
1. Reproduce chosen set of cards on sturdy cardstock.
2. Cut apart the cards and secure them with a rubber band.

Setting: Two players face each other on the floor or at a table.

How to Play:
1. Shuffle the deck of cards.
2. One player deals all cards equally to each player.
3. Players hold cards facedown in one hand. At the same time, they flip over the first card and place it faceup in front of them.
4. The card closest to "A" in alphabetical order is the winner. The player who flipped the winning card must then read both cards correctly before taking them, (e.g., "*Muffin* comes before *tomato*.").
5. You may allow words that begin with the same letter to count as "ties," to be settled as in War. Each player places one more card facedown and another faceup. The winning card is the new face-up word that is closest to "A" in alphabetical order.
6. Continue until all cards have been used once.
7. Count cards to see who won, or continue play until one player has all the cards.

Published by Frank Schaffer Publications.
Copyright protected.

0-7682-3412-3
101 Easy Reading Games

Card Games

 **Word Rummy**

Objective: introduce and reinforce three-letter words that are not short vowel words

Materials: sturdy cardstock, paper cutter, rubber bands, any type of word cards (pages 89–115, see list below)

Word Cards for Use with Word Rummy

"BR" Cards (89–90)
"FR" Cards (91–92)
"GR" Cards (93)
"TR" Cards (94)
"CR" Cards (95)
"PL" Cards (96)
"SL" Cards (97)
"SM" and "SN" Cards (98)
"SK," "SP," "SQ," "ST," and "SW" Cards (99–100)
"NG" Cards (101)
Number Word cards (103)
Animal Word cards (106–107)
Food Word cards (110–111)
Sight Word cards (112–115)

Getting Ready:
1. Reproduce three types of word cards on sturdy cardstock.
2. Cut apart all three sets of cards and secure them with a rubber band.

Setting: Two to three students play at a table or on the floor.

How to Play:
1. Shuffle the cards.
2. Deal seven cards to each player and place the rest of the cards in a facedown pile.
3. Players take turns drawing the top card on the deck or the last card discarded faceup.
4. The object is to make two sets of three cards with one of the following:
   same consonant blend
   same vowel sound
   same word family
   same category (i.e., food, animal, or number)
5. When a player can make two sets of three cards, he discards the seventh card.
6. To win, a player must explain how the sets are alike and read all six words.

Alternate Version: Play Rummy with other sets of cards, following the same rules as above or rules more applicable to the chosen set.

Silly Stories

The Silly Stories in this section are played the same way as other fill-in-the-blank activities such as Mad Libs. Review word categories with students before playing, and, if you wish, make word lists for each of the categories used: relatives, person/people, names, things, colors, days and months, animals, body parts, food, actions, and numbers.

 ## Silly Stories in a Crowd

Objective: introduce and reinforce words in common categories

Materials: Silly Stories (pages 53–57), pencil

Getting Ready: Reproduce one Silly Story three times.

Setting: Students gather around the board.

How to Play:
1. Have a volunteer fill in the blanks with words as you ask for them. (e.g., "Give me a color, number, and so on.")
2. Repeat two more times, filling in the blanks of the same story with input from different students.
3. Read aloud all versions of the story.
4. Compare the stories
   - Which parts were funny?
   - Which words made the stories funny?
   - Were their stories fantasy or reality?
   - Did any of the story elements change? If so, which ones?

 ## Silly Stories Partnerships

Objective: introduce and reinforce words in common categories

Materials: Silly Stories (pages 53–57)

Getting Ready: Reproduce enough stories that each player will get one.

Setting: Pairs of students meet in a place where one of them can write.

How to Play:
1. One person reads and fills in the blanks as directed by his partner.
2. Any words (from the given categories) may be used to fill in the blanks.
3. When the blanks are filled in, the scribe reads the story to his partner.
4. Meet in a large group, and have students read the stories to each other.

Name_____ Date_____

Silly Story # 1

The Bird Nest

One day _____ found a bird nest in a
(name)

_____. The nest was made of _____ and
(noun/thing)   (nouns/things)

_____. There were _____ eggs in the
(nouns/things)   (describing word)

_____, _____ nest. They were
(describing word)   (describing word)

_____ and about the size of a _____. We
(describing word)   (noun/thing)

did not _____ the eggs. We knew they would
(verb/action)

_____ if we _____ them.
(verb/action)   (-ed verb/action)

Name_____ Date_____

Silly Story #2

A Good Dog

One day last summer, I went to a _____ beach near
                                            (describing word)

_____. The sand felt _____ under my feet.
(noun/place)   (describing word)

The _____ was very _____. In the
    (noun/thing)   (describing word)

sky, there were _____ clouds. Some _____
                (number)   (nouns/animals)

flew overhead while I built a _____. A _____
                       (noun/thing)   (describing word)

turtle crawled slowly across the _____. Suddenly, a
                         (noun/place)

_____ dog ran into the water! A _____ boy
(describing word)   (describing word)

had fallen into the water. The _____ dog saved him.
                    (describing word)

What a good dog!

Name_____ Date_____

Silly Story #3

If I Had a Fish

If I had a fish, I would name it _____. It would live in
                                    (name)

a fish _____ in my _____. Each
          (noun/thing)   (noun/thing)

day, I would always feed it _____. It might
                              (nouns/things)

grow to be _____ _____ long and have big
              (number)   (unit of measure)

_____. My fish would be _____ with
  (nouns/things)   (describing word)

_____ spots. It would not go to _____ with
(describing word)   (noun/place)

me, but I could always tell it about what we _____.
                                               (-ed verb/action)

Name_____ Date_____

Silly Story #4

My City

I live in a _____ city. Every day I can see some
              (describing word)

_____. My city always sounds very _____.
  (nouns/things)   (describing word)

In the park I can play on _____, _____,
                       (nouns/things)   (nouns/things)

and _____. When my _____ plays with
    (nouns/things)   (noun/thing)

me there, we like to hide in the _____ and climb on
                         (noun/place)

the _____. In the city there is also a _____
   (nouns/things)   (noun/thing)

to swim in and a nice _____ to ride. In the summer
               (noun/thing)

I like to eat _____ and watch the _____
        (nouns/things)   (nouns/things)

floating on the city lake. They are _____ and
                       (describing word)

_____.
(describing word)

Published by Frank Schaffer Publications.
Copyright protected.

0-7682-3412-3
101 Easy Reading Games

Name_____ Date_____

Silly Story #5

Under the Bridge

A _____ bridge is near my _____. It is
  (describing word)   (noun/place)

_____ and _____ under the bridge. Many
(describing word)   (describing word)

_____ flowers grow there in the _____.
(describing word)   (noun/thing)

Some days I see a _____ _____
                  (describing word)   (noun/animal)

sitting on a large, _____ rock. Some _____
                (describing word)   (describing word)

_____ like to swim in the _____ water
(nouns/animals)   (describing word)

underneath the _____. Sometimes my _____
           (noun/place)   (noun/person)

takes a walk with me there and we hear a _____
                                      (noun/thing)

chirping in the _____ under the bridge.
          (noun/thing)

Silly Stories

 **Silly Story Fairy Tales and Fables**

Objective: reinforce categories of words

Materials: Silly Fairy Tales/Fables (pages 59–61)

Getting Ready: Choose one of the Silly Fairy Tales/Fables and reproduce it three times.

How to Play:
1. Three times, have students give you the words needed to rewrite the nursery rhyme.
2. After all three new versions are created, read them aloud.

 **Triple Silly Story Time**

Objective: introduce and reinforce categories of words

Materials: Silly Fairy Tales/Fables (pages 59–61)

Getting Ready: Reproduce the three pages, enough that each set of three students will receive a different one.

Setting: Three students meet in a place where one of them can write.

How to Play:
1. One person reads and fills in the blanks in one of the stories, as directed by a partner.
2. When the blanks are filled in, the scribe reads the new story to his partners.
3. Switch; another person fills in blanks of another story, as dictated by a partner, and then reads the new one.
4. When all three stories have been rewritten, meet in a large group.
5. Read aloud the original tales.
6. Next, have each student read his Silly Story to the class.

Published by Frank Schaffer Publications.
Copyright protected.

0-7682-3412-3
101 Easy Reading Games

Name_____ Date_____

Silly Fairy Tale/Fable #1

Goldilocks and the Three Bears

One day, Goldilocks was _____ in the woods. She saw
(-ing verb/action)

a _____ and decided to go in. Luckily the three
(noun/thing)

_____ who lived there were not at home. On the kitchen
(nouns/animals)

_____, she found _____ bowls of _____.
(noun/thing)   (describing word)   (nouns/things)

She tasted all of them. The last one was just right, so she ate it.

Next she went to the _____, where she saw
(noun/place)

_____ rocking _____. She sat on all of them.
(number)   (nouns/things)

One was just right, but it broke when she sat on it! She got up

and went to the _____. There, she saw _____
(noun/place)   (number)

beds. She laid on all of them. The _____ one was just
(describing word)

right. Soon, she fell asleep. When the owners came home,

Goldilocks was afraid! She _____ out of bed, ran
(-ed verb/action)

away, and never went back.

Lesson: Always respect the _____ of others.
(nouns/things)

Published by Frank Schaffer Publications.
Copyright protected.

0-7682-3412-3
101 Easy Reading Games

Silly Fairy Tale/Fable #2

The Tortoise and the Hare

Once there was a hare who loved to tease his friend the

tortoise. He would say, "You are so _____, even the

(describing word)

_____ run faster than you!" One day, the tortoise

(nouns/things)

challenged the hare to a race. The _____ hare

(describing word)

laughed. He said, "That is easy! I could win with my

_____ closed." They agreed to race the next day.

(nouns/things)

"Ready, set, go!" The tortoise took one step. The hare took

off _____. After _____ minutes, the hare was

(-ing verb/action)   (number)

far ahead. He couldn't see the tortoise, so he took a little nap.

In the mean time, the tortoise did not give up. He just kept

_____, slow and steady. The hare woke up just in time

(-ing verb/action)

to watch the tortoise _____ across the finish line.

(verb/action)

Lesson: _____ and _____ wins the race.

(describing word)   (describing word)

Name_____ Date_____

Silly Fairy Tale/Fable #3

The Boy Who Cried Wolf

Once there was a shepherd boy who loved to play jokes on people. One day, he got an idea. "Help! Help!" he yelled. "A

_____ is chasing my flock of _____!"
(noun/animal)   (nouns/animals)

The boy's friends came _____ to help him. When
(-ing verb/action)

they got there, they found out it was a joke. "That was not a

_____ joke," they said. The boy just _____.
(describing word)   (-ed verb/action)

The next day, the boy played the same joke. His friends

came _____ again. They were _____ when
(-ing verb/action)   (describing word)

they found out it was another joke. "It will not be so _____
(describing word)

when you really need our _____," they said.
(noun/thing)

Their words came true the next day. "Help! Help!" yelled

the boy. This time, a real wolf was _____ his flock!
(-ing verb/action)

No one came to help. He learned about lying the hard way!

Lesson: People don't believe liars, even when they tell the truth.

Published by Frank Schaffer Publications.
Copyright protected.
0-7682-3412-3
101 Easy Reading Games

Anytime Brain Builders

 **I Spy**

Objective: reinforce decoding skills, sight words, and drawing conclusions

Materials: none

Getting Ready: none

Setting: anywhere

How to Play: As a quick, fun, and easy way to reinforce reading skills during transition times, while standing in line, or any time you have a few spare minutes, play I Spy with vocabulary, decoding, or sight words your class is working on.

1. Begin by spotting a word in the environment that you can use as your mystery word.
2. Say, "I spy a word that..." and go on to describe something about the word (e.g., "is a synonym for *happy*," "begins with a 'br' blend," or "names an animal with scaly skin").
3. Students look around at the environmental print and take turns guessing.
4. The first student to guess it correctly must also correctly point toward it. If he can do so, he takes the next turn. Continue this way for as long as time allows.

 **I'm Thinking of Something**

Objective: reinforce phonemic awareness, decoding, vocabulary, and comprehension skills

Materials: none

Getting Ready: none

Setting: anywhere

How to Play: This game is another versatile and easy way to reinforce reading skills any time and anyplace.

1. Begin by thinking of a word or concept that you can use as your mystery word or phrase.
2. Say, "I'm thinking of..." and go on to describe something about the word (see examples below).
3. Students take turns guessing.

4. The first student to guess it correctly takes the next turn. Continue this way for as long as time allows.

Examples:

- <u>Phonemic Awareness:</u> "a word with three syllables," "an animal that rhymes with *peel*"
- <u>Decoding:</u> "a word that starts with a 'tr' blend," "a word with a long 'a' sound"
- <u>Vocabulary:</u> "a homophone that means *calm* or *a part*," "a compound word you can wear in the water"
- <u>Comprehension:</u> "the problem in *The Gingerbread Man*," "something that causes a broken window"
- <u>Combined Skills:</u> "a synonym for *job* that has a short 'a' sound"

Anytime Brain Builders

61 I Spy "GN" and "QU" Words

Objective: introduce and reinforce words with initial letter combinations "gn" and "qu"—gnash, gnarl, gnome, gnaw, gnats, quack, quail, queen, question, quick, quicksand, quiet, quilt, quit, quite

Materials: "GN" and "QU" word list and clue list (page 64)

Getting Ready: Copy page 64 onto an overhead transparency or copy the "gn" and "qu" words somewhere visible to all players.

Setting: Students meet in a large informal group.

How to Play: Read the word list together as a group. If working with an overhead transparency, cover the clues with a sheet of paper so they do not project onto the screen. Read one word clue off the list as students take turns guessing. Repeat for each clue. (Explain that a word may be used more than one time in the game.)

62 I'm Thinking of "WH" Words

Objective: introduce and reinforce words that begin with "wh"—whale, what, wheat, wheel, when, where, which, whiff, while, whim, whine, whip, whirl, whisper, whistle, white, whiz, who, whom, whole

Materials: "WH" word list and clue list (page 65)

Getting Ready: Copy page 65 onto an overhead transparency or copy the "wh" words somewhere visible to all players.

Setting: Students meet in a large informal group.

How to Play: Read the word list together as a group. If working with an overhead transparency, cover the clues with a sheet of paper so they do not project onto the screen. Read one word clue off the list as students take turns guessing. Repeat for each clue. (Explain that a word may be used more than one time in the game.)

63 Mystery "PR" Words

Objective: introduce and reinforce words that begin with "pr"—practice, praise, prance, prank, prepare, press, pretend, pretty, price, pride, prince, princess, principal, print, prize, program, project, promise, prove, prune

Materials: "PR" word list and clue list (page 66)

Getting Ready: Copy page 66 onto an overhead transparency or copy the "pr" words somewhere visible to all players.

Setting: Students meet in a large informal group.

How to Play: Read the word list together as a group. If working with an overhead transparency, cover the clues with a sheet of paper so they do not project onto the screen. Read one word clue off the list as students take turns guessing. Repeat for each clue. (Explain that a word may be used more than one time in the game.)

I Spy "GN" and "QU" Words

gnash	gnarl	gnome	gnaw	gnat
quack	quail	queen	question	quick
quicksand	quiet	quilt	quit	quite

1. I spy a word that rhymes with *thaw*. (gnaw)
2. I spy something that keeps you warm. (quilt)
3. I spy a word that rhymes with *home*. (gnome)
4. I spy a word that rhymes with *try it*. (quiet)
5. I spy a word that means *fast*. (quick)
6. I spy a word that rhymes with *crash*. (gnash)
7. I spy a word that rhymes with *sit*. (quit)
8. I spy a word that means "twisted." (snarl)
9. I spy a word that rhymes with *flick*. (quick)
10. I spy a kind of bird. (quail)
11. I spy something dangerous to step into. (quicksand)
12. I spy a word that rhymes with *command*. (quicksand)
13. I spy a kind of sentence that asks. (question)
14. I spy a royal person. (queen)
15. I spy a small creature from fairy tales. (gnome)
16. I spy a silent classroom. (quiet)
17. I spy a word that means "to grind." (gnash)
18. I spy a word that means "to chew." (gnaw)
19. I spy an animal sound. (quack)
20. I spy a very small insect. (gnat)

Published by Frank Schaffer Publications.
Copyright protected.

0-7682-3412-3
101 Easy Reading Games

I'm Thinking of "WH" Words

whale	what	wheat	wheel	when
whale	what	wheat	wheel	when
where	which	whiff	while	whim
whine	whip	whirl	whisper	whistle
white	whiz	who	whom	whole

1. I'm thinking of the largest mammal. (whale)
2. I'm thinking of a word asked to find a place. (where)
3. I'm thinking of an annoying sound. (whine)
4. I'm thinking of something round. (wheel)
5. I'm thinking of receiving a small amount of a smell. (whiff)
6. I'm thinking of a word that rhymes with *smile.* (while)
7. I'm thinking of something use to make bread. (wheat)
8. I'm thinking of something done to cream. (whip)
9. I'm thinking of a word asked to discover a thing. (what)
10. I'm thinking of another word for *twirl.* (whirl)
11. I'm thinking of a word asked to find out a cause. (why)
12. I'm thinking of a word asked to discover one of several things. (which)
13. I'm thinking of a musical sound you make by blowing. (whistle)
14. I'm thinking of someone who is very fast or smart. (whiz)
15. I'm thinking of a word asked to discover a time. (when)
16. I'm thinking of a three-letter word asked to discover a person. (who)
17. I'm thinking of a color. (white)
18. I'm thinking of a way to talk quietly. (whisper)
19. I'm thinking of the opposite of "a piece." (whole)
20. I'm thinking of a four-letter word asked to talk about a person. (whom)

Published by Frank Schaffer Publications.

0-7682-3412-3
101 Easy Reading Games

Mystery "PR" Words

practice	praise	prance	prank	prepare
press	pretend	pretty	price	pride
prince	princess	principal	print	prize
program	project	promise	prove	prune

1. How does a horse move? (prance)
2. What is something you win in a contest? (prize)
3. What is a vow you make to someone? (promise)
4. What is something one gives another when they like what they are doing? (praise)
5. What is something you must do to get good at playing a musical instrument? (practice)
6. If you are not guilty, you must _____ you are innocent. (prove)
7. What is a dried plum? (prune)
8. What is a trick people play? (prank)
9. What is another way of saying "get ready"? (prepare)
10. What is something a student does for science class? (project)
11. What is another word for *beautiful*? (pretty)
12. What do you do to a doorbell? (press)
13. What do you do when you make believe? (pretend)
14. The cost of something is the _____ . (price)
15. Feeling good about one's self is to have _____ . (pride)
16. Another word for a concert or show is a _____ . (program)
17. To write words with a pencil is to _____ . (print)
18. List two words that describe people. (pretty, proud)
19. List three people words. (prince, princess, principal)
20. List six action words. (any of the following: practice, praise, prance, pray, prefer, prepare, press, pretend, print, program, promise, prove, provide, prune)

Anytime Brain Builders

 **20 Questions**

Objective: reinforce vocabulary and comprehension skills

Materials: none

Getting Ready: none

Setting: anywhere

How to Play: This game is another versatile and easy way to reinforce reading skills any time and anyplace.

1. Begin by thinking of a word or concept that you can use as your mystery word or phrase.

2. Say, "I'm thinking of…" and give one clue about the word (e.g., a homonym, a compound word, a character, and so on).

3. Students take turns asking *yes* or *no* questions about the word. The players are allowed unlimited *yes* answers, but only 20 *no* answers.

4. The first student to guess the word correctly takes the next turn. If nobody guesses correctly with 20 or fewer "no" answers, reveal the answer and begin again with a new word. Continue this way for as long as time allows.

 **Say It Again**

Objective: practice phonemic awareness skills

Materials: none

Getting Ready: none

Setting: anywhere

How to Play:

1. Choose any word. You may wish to play with mixed word and skill types or focus on a specific type of phoneme (e.g., initial consonants/blends, suffixes, or syllables—see examples below). Tell players, "Say (the word)."

2. Players say the word.

3. Tell the players, "Say it again, but don't say (one phoneme/part of the word)."

4. Repeat for as many words as you want to work on, playing for points if you wish.

Examples:
- Compound Words: "Say *mailbox*. Say it again but don't say *box*." (mail)
- Initial Consonants/Blends: "Say *black*. Say it again but don't say *ack*." (bl)
- Final Consonants/Blends: "Say *beast*. Say it again but don't say *st*." (bea)
- Prefixes/Suffixes: "Say *redo*. Say it again but don't say *re*." (do)
- Syllables: "Say *popsicle*. Say it again but don't say *sic*." (pop-le)
- Vowel Sounds/Blends: "Say *tree*. Say it again but don't say *ee*. (tr)

Published by Frank Schaffer Publications.
Copyright protected.

0-7682-3412-3
101 Easy Reading Games

Anytime Brain Builders

 **Short Vowel Crossword**

Objective: review three-letter short vowel words

Materials: Crossword Spelling Game Board (page 69), pencils, stopwatch

Getting Ready: Reproduce a Crossword page for each pair of students.

Setting: Pairs sit at a table beside each other.

How to Play:
1. Players cooperate to fill every space on their crossword by printing short vowel words. The words must read across and down.

2. In five minutes, see how many short vowel words students can print on their cards.

Possible Answers:
- bad, fad, lad, mad, pad, sad, tad, bag, gag, lag, rag, wag, ban, can, fan, man, pan, bat, cat, fat, hat, mat, pat, rat, sat, cab, gab, jab, lab, nab, am, clam, dam, ham, jam, lamb, ram
- beg, keg, leg, bet, get, let, met, net, pet, set, vet, yet, den, hen, men, pen, ten
- big, dig, fig, jig, pig, rig, wig, bin, fin, pin, tin, win, bit, fit, hit, kit, pit, sit, wit
- cob, rob, sob, cot, dot, got, hot, jot, not, rot, cop, hop, mop, top
- bug, dug, hug, jug, lug, sub, tub

 Blend Word Categories

Objective: reinforce words with consonant blends

Materials: Blend Word Categories activity sheet (page 70), pencils, dictionaries

Getting Ready:
1. Reproduce the Blend Word Categories page (page 70) for each student.
2. Copy page 70 onto an overhead transparency or copy the blends and word endings somewhere visible to all players.

Setting: Students sit at desks or a table with a work surface.

How to Play:
1. Pass out the activity sheets to students and set a reasonable time limit (about 15 or 20 minutes).
2. Students race to list initial consonant blends with the endings on the cards.
3. They may use dictionaries to check spellings.
4. Every correct word they list is five points. Every incorrect word is minus five points.
5. When time is called, have students share answers and list them on the overhead.
6. The players with the most real words listed are declared the winners. (For answer suggestions, see words on page 102.)

Alternate Version: Instead of playing for a given time, see who can list 75 words first.

Published by Frank Schaffer Publications.
Copyright protected.

0-7682-3412-3
101 Easy Reading Games

Name_____ Date_____

Crossword Spelling Game Board

Published by Frank Schaffer Publications.
Copyright protected.

0-7682-3412-3
101 Easy Reading Games

Blend Word Categories

Directions: Use the blends from the boxes to make words with the endings below. Make as many real words as you can in the time you are given.

bl	cl	fl	gl	pl	sl	br	cr	dr	fr
gr	pr	tr	sm	sn	st	sw	sk	sp	spr

-ace _____

-aid _____

-ain _____

-an _____

-ane _____

-ank _____

-ant _____

-ate _____

-ay _____

-ead _____

-ease _____

-edge _____

-enty _____

-od _____

-ot _____

-ow _____

-ug _____

-um _____

-us _____

-oom _____

Anytime Brain Builders

68 Reverse Blend Word Categories

Objective: reinforce words with consonant blends

Materials: white board, list of blends you want to work on, stopwatch

Getting Ready: Divide the students into teams of four to six members.

Setting: Teams gather at the board.

How to Play:
1. The first player from each team stands at the board.
2. Name a blend.
3. Players have 60 seconds to list as many words with that initial blend as they can.
4. Each correct word a player lists is a point for his team.
5. As you play, keep score on the board.

69 Other Categories

Objective: demonstrate ability to generate words with given sounds or syllables, details for a given main idea, story elements, synonyms, vocabulary that fits a given profile, causes and effects, or facts and opinions

Materials: white board, list of reading skills or words you want to work on, stopwatch

Getting Ready: Divide the students into teams of four to six members.

Setting: Teams gather at the board.

How to Play:
1. The first player from each team stands at the board.
2. Name a category.
3. Players have sixty seconds to list as many words in that category as they can.
4. Each correct word a player lists is a point for his team.
5. As you play, keep score on the board.

Examples:

Words with given sounds or syllables: -ing words, long "a" words, short "o" words, words from the "-ale" word family, animals beginning with "r," words with two syllables

Details for a given main idea: feelings, calendar words, healthy foods, toys, birds, things you might find in a city, community helpers, things you do when you're happy

Story Elements: animal character names, fantasy settings, problems involving school

Vocabulary: compound words, words with "ball" in them, homophone sets, antonym pairs, actions words (verbs), describing words (adjectives), plural nouns, words that could describe rotting food, science vocabulary words

Published by Frank Schaffer Publications.
Copyright protected.

0-7682-3412-3
101 Easy Reading Games

Anytime Brain Builders

 **Beat the Clock**

Objective: develop fluency with basic sight words

Materials: Sight Word cards (pages 112–115), sturdy cardstock, paper cutter, rubber bands, stopwatch

Getting Ready:
1. Reproduce the Sight Word cards for each member of your group.
2. Cut apart the cards and secure each deck with a rubber band.
3. Give each student a deck of Sight Word cards.

Setting: Pairs of students sit at a table facing each other.

How to Play:
1. Shuffle the deck of Sight Word cards.
2. As the teacher times one minute, one player in each pair flashes the cards as quickly as possible to the partner.
3. At the end of one minute, time is called.
4. Count how many cards the player read.
5. Repeat with the partner reading the cards.
6. At the end of one minute, count how many cards the player read.
7. Help students total the scores to see which pair wins.

 Beat the Clock Reading Relay

Objective: develop fluency with basic sight words

Materials: Sight Word cards (pages 112–115)

Getting Ready: Reproduce or locate one set of Sight Word cards.

Setting: Teams line up near board.

How to Play:
1. Divide the class into two teams and have the team members line up one behind another. Shuffle the deck of Sight Word cards.
2. As the teacher times three minutes, she flashes the cards to one member after another (relay fashion).
3. At the end of three minutes, time is called.
4. Count how many cards the team read.
5. Repeat with the other team.
6. The team with the most cards read wins.

 **Beat the Clock Blends**

Objective: develop fluency with various blend words

Materials: any of the word cards with blends (pages 89–101)

Getting Ready: Reproduce or locate the word cards you want to use.

Setting: Teams line up near the board.

How to Play:
Play as Beat the Clock or Beat the Clock Reading Relay above.

Published by Frank Schaffer Publications.
Copyright protected.

0-7682-3412-3
101 Easy Reading Games

Anytime Brain Builders

73 Sort and Count

Objective: introduce and reinforce words that begin with "sk," "sp," "sq," "st," and "sw" blends

Materials: "SK," "SP," "SQ," "ST," and "SW" cards (pages 99–100), paper cutter, rubber bands

Getting Ready:
1. Reproduce a set of cards for each pair of students.
2. Cut apart the cards and secure each deck with a rubber band.
3. Pair students and give each pair a deck of cards.

Setting: Students gather on the floor or outside on the grass.

How to Play: Give directions as pairs cooperate to find the answers. Each pair must show the cards to win the point for that round. As you play, keep score.

1. How many words have a short "i" sound? (11—skin, skinny, skip, spill, spin, stiff, still, stint, string, swift, swim)
2. How many words begin with "sk"? (5—skate, skin, skinny, skip, skunk)
3. How many words have a short "e" sound? (4—spell, stegosaurus, step, strength)
4. How many words begin with "sw"? (11—swallow, swan, swap, sweet, swift, swim, swing, swam, sweep, swat, sway)
5. How many words have a short "a" sound? (2—splash, swam)
6. How many words begin with "st"? (20—stale, start, state, station, stay, stegosaurus, step, stiff, still, stint, stock, stream, street, strength, string, stripe, stroke, struggle, study, stuff)
7. How many words have a short "o" sound? (2—stock, spot)
8. How many words have a long "a" sound? (7—skate, space, stale, state, station, stay, sway)
9. How many words begin with "squ"? (4—squash, square, squeeze, squirt)
10. How many words have a short "u" sound? (4—skunk, struggle, study, stuff)
11. How many words have a long "e" sound? (6—speak, squeeze, stream, street, sweep, sweet)
12. How many words begin with "sp"? (12—skip, skunk, space, speak, spell, spill, spin, splash, spoke, spoon, sport, spot)
13. How many words have a long "i" sound? (1—stripe)
14. How many words have a long "o" sound? (2—spoke, stroke)
15. How many words have a long "u" sound? (0)

Published by Frank Schaffer Publications.
Copyright protected.

0-7682-3412-3
101 Easy Reading Games

Anytime Brain Builders

 **Find and Respond "TR" Trains**

Objective: develop memory skills and fluency with "tr" blend words

Materials: "TR" Word cards (page 94), white board (or overhead, chalkboard, or chart paper), cardstock, paper cutter, rubber bands

Getting Ready:
1. Reproduce, cut, and gather with a rubber band a set of cards for each student.
2. Give each student a set of cards and read the words together.

Setting: Students sit at desks or tables with a working surface.

How to Play:
1. Name three "tr" words.
2. Students make a "train" of the word cards in the order they hear them. When the "word train" is made, students raise hands.
3. Roam the classroom checking "trains."
4. Advance to naming four or five "tr" words for students to line up in order.
5. Increase the number of words to six or seven.

75 Find and Respond "CR" or "TR" Word

Objective: introduce and reinforce words with initial "cr" and "tr" blends

Materials: "CR" Word cards and "TR" Word cards (pages 95 and 94), cardstock, paper cutter, rubber bands

Getting Ready:
1. Reproduce, cut, and gather with a rubber band a set of cards for each student.
2. Review the blend sounds "cr" and "tr."

Setting: Students sit on the floor or outside on the grass with their deck of word cards.

How to Play:
1. One at a time, say a word.
2. Students respond with the initial blend sound in one of two ways:
   • "cr"—crow like a rooster
   • "tr"—trumpet like an elephant
3. After everyone responds with a sound, students race to find the card and hold it up.

 Find and Respond Other Blends

Objective: introduce and reinforce words with consonant blends

Materials: any consonant blend word cards, cardstock, paper cutter, rubber bands

Getting Ready:
1. Reproduce, cut, and gather with a rubber band a set of cards for each student.

2. Review the blend sounds you are going to learn.

Setting: Students sit on the floor or outside on the grass with their deck of word cards.

How to Play: Play as Find and Respond above. Substitute different responses for crowing and trumpeting.

Published by Frank Schaffer Publications.
Copyright protected.

0-7682-3412-3
101 Easy Reading Games

Anytime Brain Builders

Sentence Building: Sentences Under Construction

Objective: introduce and reinforce sight words

Materials: Sight Word cards (pages 112–115), paper cutter, rubber bands

Getting Ready:
1. Reproduce word cards for each group of three or four.
2. Cut apart the cards and secure each set with a rubber band.

Setting: Divide students into teams of three or four and have each team sit at a table or group themselves on the floor.

How to Play:
1. Players cooperate in using the cards to make complete sentences with at least four words. (e.g., "The teacher was willing.") They leave each sentence they make.
2. At the end of given time period, the team with the most sentences is declared the winner.

Sentence Building: Super Sentence Construction

How to Play:
Prepare and play using Sentences Under Construction directions. Set a time limit of 20 minutes. The object is to see which team can construct the longest sentence. Allow students to use articles—a, an, the, and the conjunction—and, as many times as they like.

When time is called:
- count to see which team's sentence has the most words.
- check to see which team's sentence has the most letters.
- read to see which team's sentence is the funniest (most interesting).
- declare the winning teams.

Sentence Building: Construction Card Game

Prepare cards and play using Sentences Under Construction directions. Groups of two to three play at a table or on the floor.

How to Play:
1. Deal each player ten cards.
2. Players draw and discard in turn until someone can make a sentence. The player receives the number of points as there are words in his sentence.

3. Collect cards, shuffle, and deal again.
4. Continue until one player has earned 12 points.

Published by Frank Schaffer Publications.
Copyright protected.

0-7682-3412-3
101 Easy Reading Games

Anytime Brain Builders

80 Fact or Opinion?

Objective: introduce and reinforce facts and opinions

Materials: list of statements

Getting Ready:
1. Choose a story to read aloud. If you wish, prepare fact and opinion statements about the story.
2. Teach students sign language for the letters "f" and "o."

Setting: Students sit in seats or gather in a listening area.

How to Play:
1. Read the chosen story aloud.
2. At the end of the story, state a fact or opinion.
3. Students use sign language letters to show "f" if they believe the statement is a fact and "o" if they believe it is an opinion.
4. Reveal the correct answer, and repeat with another statement. You may keep points (class vs. teacher) if you wish. You may also allow students to take turn making up the statements and revealing their answers.

81 Reality or Fantasy?

Objective: introduce and reinforce what makes a story reality or fantasy

Materials: stories or list of stories

Getting Ready:
1. Choose a story to read aloud.
2. Teach students sign language for the letters "f" and "r."

Setting: Students sit in seats or gather in a listening area.

How to Play:
1. Read the chosen story or the title of a well-known story aloud.
2. Students indicate with sign language whether the story was reality or fantasy. They use sign language letters to show "f" if they believe the story is fantasy and "r" if they believe it is reality.
3. Call on students to list details that support their answers.
4. Reveal the correct answer, and repeat with another story. You may keep points (class vs. teacher) if you wish. You may also allow students to take turns selecting stories.

Anytime Brain Builders

82 Gleeful "GL" Wheels

Objective: introduce and reinforce words that begin with the "gl" blend—*glad, glass, glaze, gleam, glean, glee, glide, glider, glitter, gloat, glob, glove, gloom, gloomy, glory, gloss, glove, glow, glowing, glue*

Materials: white board (or overhead, chalkboard, or chart paper), two pointers

Getting Ready:
1. On the board, print the "gl" blend and draw the two wheels.

Setting: Students gather at the board.

How to Play:
1. Pair students. One pair at a time holds the pointers.
2. Say a word that begins with a "gl" bend.
3. Each member of the pair points to a section on one of the wheels.
4. If the team correctly spells the word, they get a point.
5. If the team cannot point out the letters to spell the word, the pointers are handed to the next pair who tries to point it out.
6. Repeat until every team has had several turns to spell a "gl" word.
7. As you play, keep score on the board and make a list of "gl" words.

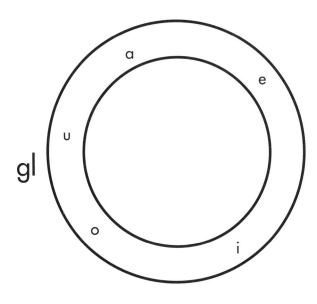

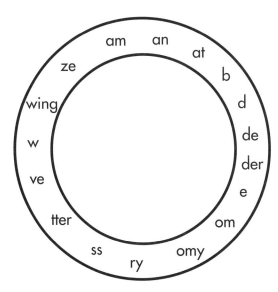

Anytime Brain Builders

 **"DR" Challenges**

Objective: introduce and reinforce words that begin with "dr" blend

Materials: white board (or overhead, chalkboard, or chart paper), "DR" Challenges

Getting Ready: Divide students into three or four teams.

Setting: A player from each team stands at the board.

How to Play:

1. Say and spell the first word as the players print it on the board.
2. Give the directions and repeat them once.
3. The first player to print the correct answer wins a point for her team.
4. Then the next member of each team comes to the board.
5. Give the second challenge.
6. As you play, keep score on the board and make a "dr" word list.

"DR" Challenges:

1. drag—Change one letter and make something a doctor gives a sick person. (drug)
2. dragon—Add an animal word and make it another animal. (dragonfly)
3. drape—Add one letter and it is something done yesterday. (draped)
4. drew—Change one letter and make it something you do in art. (draw)
5. dread—Change one letter and make it something you do at night. (dream)
6. drove—Change one letter and make it what people do with cars. (drive)
7. dream—Change one letter and make it a synonym for fear. (dread)
8. drift—Change two letters and make it how you practice for a fire. (drill)
9. drip—Change one letter and make it a small amount. (drop)
10. drum—Change one letter to make it past tense. (drove)
11. drop—Add one extra letter and make a synonym for sag. (droop)
12. dressed—Remove two letters to make a piece of clothing. (dress)
13. drink—Change one letter and make something you did with your soda. (drank)
14. droop—Drop a letter and make one word in this sentence. (drop)
15. dram—Change one vowel to two and make something that happens when you sleep. (dream)

Published by Frank Schaffer Publications.
Copyright protected.

0-7682-3412-3
101 Easy Reading Games

Anytime Brain Builders

84 Final "CH" and "SH" Relay

Objective: introduce and reinforce words that end with the "ch" or "sh" digraph—*beach, brush, crash, finish, fish, foolish, fresh, much, rush, speech, spinach, trash*

Materials: one copy of word clues, white board, overhead

Getting Ready:
1. Divide the students into three or four teams.
2. Put the word list up on the overhead.

Setting: Teams gather at the board.

How to Play: As you read from the list of clues, students go to the board and print guesses. The first to get it wins a point for his team.

"CH" and "SH" Clues:
1. used to neaten your hair (brush)
2. seashore (beach)
3. speaking (speech)
4. another way to say hurry (rush)
5. lives in water (fish)
6. vegetable (spinach)
7. to collide (crash)
8. not very clever (foolish)
9. just-picked vegetables (fresh)
10. the end (finish)
11. refuse (trash)
12. lots (much)

Published by Frank Schaffer Publications.
Copyright protected.

0-7682-3412-3
101 Easy Reading Games

Anytime Brain Builders

85 Circle Game: Main Ideas and Details

Objective: generate details to go with a given main idea

Materials: none

Getting Ready: If desired, make a list of main ideas or categories you would like to focus on with your group.

Setting: The class gathers in a circle.

How to Play:

1. The teacher or one of the players chooses a main idea or category and shares it with the group.
2. One person in the circle is chosen to go first. He must state one detail that supports the main idea. If he cannot give one, he says "pass," and play passes to the right. (If you wish, you may award points for every correct answer. You may also put a time limit on each player's turn.)
3. Play continues one full time around the circle, and a new main idea is chosen.

86 Circle Game: Causes and Effects

Objective: generate a chain of reasonable causes and effects

Materials: none

Getting Ready: If desired, make a list of causes you can use to start off the chain. (e.g., Last Friday, Bill woke up late.)

Setting: The class gathers in a circle.

How to Play:

1. The teacher or one of the players states an event that may cause something to happen. (You may use the starters from the What If cards on page 125.)
2. One person in the circle is chosen to go first. He must state one reasonable effect that may result from the given cause. If he cannot give one, he says "pass," and play passes to the right. (If you wish, you may award points for every correct answer. You may also put a time limit on each player's turn.)
3. The next player must state a reasonable cause for the event given by the player just before her (on her left).
4. Play continues one full time around the circle or until the chain of causes and effects reaches a logical conclusion.

87 Circle Game: Sequencing

Play as the Causes and Effects Circle Game above. Instead of generating a series of causes and effects, players generate a series of events that do not need to have a cause and effect relationship. Encourage players to use such sequence words as "First, Second, and Third" or "In the beginning, in the middle, and at the end."

Published by Frank Schaffer Publications.
Copyright protected.

0-7682-3412-3
101 Easy Reading Games

Kinesthetic / Moving Games

 **Run and Read Sight Words**

Objective: introduce and reinforce sight words

Materials: Sight Word cards (pages 112–115)

Getting Ready:
1. Reproduce the sight word game cards four times.
2. Cut apart the cards and secure each deck with a rubber band.
3. Divide students into four teams.

Setting: Players meet on blacktop or an open area, and each team lines up.

How to Play:
1. On the blacktop, place stacks of cards ten feet apart. (You may select 30 cards from each deck to use as more manageable word stacks.)
2. Teams line up about 20 feet from the game cards.
3. Call out a sight word.
4. The first player on each team runs to their team's game cards and flips through them to find the word. He brings it back to the teacher. The first player back wins a point for his team.
5. Say another sight word, and the second member of each team races to find it.

 **More Run and Read**

How to Play: Use the same game rules as Run and Read Sight Words to reinforce more words. Use one of the following card combinations.
- Food Word cards (pages 110–111)
- Animal Word cards (pages 106–107)
- Number Word cards (page 103)
- any of the Blend Word cards (pages 89–101)

 **Run and Read with Clues**

How to Play: Use the same game rules as Run and Read Sight Words to practice comprehension of vocabulary words. Instead of reading the word, however, give a clue about the word. You may use number, animal, or food word cards, as well as homophones, antonyms, synonyms, or compound words. Use word cards from any of the appropriate pages or create your own.

Published by Frank Schaffer Publications.
Copyright protected.

0-7682-3412-3
101 Easy Reading Games

Kinesthetic / Moving Games

91 Find Your Other Half

Objective: reinforce vocabulary knowledge and skills

Materials: sturdy cardstock, paper cutter, glue stick, any type of word cards (pages 116–119, see list below)

> **Word Cards for Use with Find Your Other Half**
> Homophone cards (116)
> Synonym cards (117)
> Antonym cards (118)
> Compound Word cards (119)

Getting Ready:
1. Reproduce one set of your chosen word cards.
2. Cut apart the cards and secure with a rubber band.

Setting: An open space where players may walk around freely.

How to Play:
1. Pass out the pairs of cards so that each player has a card that matches in some way with another player's card (e.g., small and little, sword and fish).
2. When the teacher says go, players walk around and check out each other's cards to find their match. When they find each other, they sit down.
3. The players try to beat the clock by finding every pair within a given time limit. When time runs out, all the pairs take turns reading off their words.

Alternate Version: Instead of playing with word pairs, you may play with word groups, such as words from a certain word family or words with a certain consonant blend. In this case, players find and sit together with their group rather than with a partner.

92 Animal or Food Charades

Objective: reinforce understanding of vocabulary words, practice categorization skills

Materials: Animal Word cards (pages 106–107) and/or Food Word cards (pages 110–111), scissors, paper bag

Getting Ready:
1. Reproduce either or both sets of the word cards.
2. Cut apart the cards, fold each one, and place them in a paper bag.

Setting: Students gather in a place where they can all see one player acting out a word.

How to Play:
1. Players take turns drawing a word from the bag and acting it out.
2. Others shout out their guesses.
3. The first person to shout out the correct word must then identify the category it came from (animal or food). If he does name the correct category, it is his turn to act. If not, continue calling on players until someone correctly names the category.
4. Continue taking turns drawing until all cards have been used.

Published by Frank Schaffer Publications.
Copyright protected.

0-7682-3412-3
101 Easy Reading Games

Kinesthetic / Moving Games

 **Sight Word Charades**

Objective: reinforce understanding of vocabulary sight words

Materials: Sight Word cards (pages 112–115), scissors, paper bag

Getting Ready:
1. Reproduce the word cards. Remove any words you feel would be too complicated for students to act out (e.g., *does, must, was, were,* and so on).
2. Cut apart the cards, fold each one, and place them in a paper bag.

Setting: Students gather in a place where they can all see one player acting out a word.

How to Play:
1. Players take turns drawing a word from the bag and acting out the word.
2. Others shout out their guesses.
3. The first person to shout out the correct word must then spell it correctly. If he does spell it correctly, it is his turn to act out a word. If not, continue calling on players until someone correctly spells the word.
4. Continue taking turns drawing until all cards have been used or you run out of time.

 **Compound Word Charades**

Objective: reinforce understanding of compound words

Materials: Compound Word cards (page 119), scissors, paper bag

Getting Ready:
1. Reproduce the word cards.
2. Cut apart the cards, fold each one, and place them in a paper bag.

Setting: Students gather in a place where they can all see one player acting out a word.

How to Play:
1. Players take turns drawing a compound word from the bag and acting out the word. This may be one action that represents the whole word or two separate actions that represent each smaller word (e.g., *bookworm* could either be acted out as a bookworm, or as a book and a worm).
2. Others shout out their guesses.
3. The first person to shout out the correct word must then identify the two smaller words that make up the compound word. If she does correctly identify them, it is her turn to act. If not, continue calling on players until someone correctly names the two smaller words.
4. Continue taking turns drawing until all the cards have been used or you are out of time.

Kinesthetic / Moving Games

 **Homophone Charades**

Objective: reinforce understanding of homophones

Materials: Homophone cards (page 116), scissors, paper bag

Getting Ready:
1. Reproduce the word cards.
2. Cut apart the cards, fold each one, and place them in a paper bag.

Setting: Students gather in a place where they can all see one player acting out a word.

How to Play:
1. Players take turns drawing a homophone from the bag and acting it out.
2. Others shout out their guesses.

3. The first person to shout out the correct word must then give the definition and spell it correctly. If he does both correctly, it is his turn to draw. If not, continue calling on players until someone answers correctly.
4. Continue taking turns drawing until all cards have been used or you are out of time.

Alternate Version: In addition to spelling and defining the word once it is guessed, you may have the player who is guessing state the homophone's pair and definition (e.g., for *see*, the player would also have to name and define *sea*).

 Synonym or Antonym Charades

Objective: reinforce understanding of synonyms and antonyms

Materials: Synonym cards (page 117), Antonym cards (page 118), scissors, paper bag

Getting Ready:
1. Reproduce the word cards.
2. Cut apart the cards, fold each one, and place them in a paper bag.

Setting: Students gather in a place where they can all see one player acting out a word.

How to Play:
1. Players take turns drawing a synonym or antonym card from the bag and acting it out.
2. Others shout out their guesses.
3. The first person to shout out the correct answer must then name the correct synonym or antonym of the acted word. If he names it correctly, it is his turn to act. If not, continue calling on players until someone answers correctly.
4. Continue taking turns drawing until all cards have been used or you are out of time.

Published by Frank Schaffer Publications.
Copyright protected.

0-7682-3412-3
101 Easy Reading Games

Kinesthetic / Moving Games

 **Story Element Charades**

Objective: introduce and reinforce story elements

Materials: paper, scissors, paper bag, two-minute timer

Getting Ready:
1. On slips of paper, write down titles of stories your students have read.
2. Place the titles in a paper bag.
3. Divide students into two teams.

Setting: Students gather at the board.

How to Play:
1. Establish which story element you will be focusing on in your game (characters, setting, problem, solution, or events). Here are four ways to decide:
   - Focus on one story element for the whole game.
   - Play in rounds, with each round dedicated to a different story element.
   - With each draw, use a die or spinner marked with the story elements to determine the category.

2. Students take turns drawing a card from the bag.
3. A player has two minutes to act out the designated story element of that story.
4. Students take turns shouting out guesses when their team is drawing.
5. When a team guesses correctly within the time limit, they get a point and another turn. If the team does not guess correctly, the other team has a chance to guess and "steal" the point. It is then the other team's turn to act.

Alternate Version: Instead of writing down story titles, have students fill out the Story Element Graphic Organizer from page 9. Use these as the "cards" players draw and act out.

Kinesthetic / Moving Games

 **Scavenger Hunt**

Objective: practice finding and recognizing words in the environment

Materials: list of words to find (see Getting Ready below), pencils

Getting Ready:
1. Create a list of words or clues to words you want students to find. Make sure the words are posted somewhere in the environment.
2. Make one copy of the list for each student or group of students if you will be playing in partners or teams.

Setting: Students search an area designated by the teacher.

How to Play:
1. Break students into teams or tell them they will be playing as individuals.
2. Pass out the word lists. Explain to students that the words on the list can be found in the environment.
3. Set a time limit and allow students to search the environment for the given amount of time.
4. At the end of the time, gather together and count up totals to see who has found the most words. The student or team with the most words wins if they can point out each word to the group.

 **Clambake**

Objective: introduce and reinforce words that begin with "cl" blend—*clam, clamp, clan, clang, clap, clash, clasp, claw, clay, clean, clear, cleat, clerk, clever, click, climb, clinch, cling, clip, clock, close, cloth, cloud, clown, club, clue, clump*

Materials: construction paper, clam patterns (page 87), marker, "cl" word list above, sandbox, or other outdoor spot for hiding clams

Getting Ready:
1. On white construction paper, reproduce the clam pattern page five times. Cut out the clams.
2. On each clam, print one of the following: *am, amp, an, ang, ap, ash, asp, aw, ay, ean, ear, eat, erk, ever, ick, imb, inch, ing, ip, ock, ose, oth, oud, own, ub, ue, ump.*

3. Just before the game, hide the clams in the sand or other place on the playground.

Setting: Students gather outside in a sandbox (to suggest the beach), on the grass, or some similar place.

How to Play:
1. Explain that you have hidden the clams and that each student is to try to find one.
2. When a player finds a clam, he returns to a designated spot and shouts out the word made by the "cl" blend and the letters on his clam.
3. When all the students have reassembled, take turns reading the "cl" blend words.

Published by Frank Schaffer Publications.
Copyright protected.

0-7682-3412-3
101 Easy Reading Games

Kinesthetic / Moving Games

Clam Patterns

Kinesthetic / Moving Games

 **Body Language**

Objective: introduce and reinforce "br," "fr," and "sl" words

Materials: word cards (pages 89–92 and 97), scissors, paper bag

Getting Ready:
1. Reproduce the word cards.
2. Cut apart the cards and fold each once.
3. Place the cards in a paper bag.

Setting: Students gather at the board.

How to Play:
1. Students take turns drawing a word from the bag.
2. When they are "it," they write the word they chose on their forearm with their finger, holding it out so that the other students can watch.
3. Students shout out their guesses.
4. The first player to correctly guess the word gets to draw the next card from the bag.

Alternate Version: Water Writing
Play the same way as Body Language above, but play outside. Instead of writing words on their forearms, players use paintbrushes dipped in water to write words on concrete surfaces.

 **Shadow Writing**

Objective: introduce and reinforce "cr" and "tr" words

Materials: word cards (pages 94 and 95), scissors, paper bag

Getting Ready:
1. Reproduce the word cards.
2. Cut apart the cards and fold each once.
3. Place the cards in a paper bag.
4. Divide the players into three or four teams.

Setting: Play outside on a sunny day, while there are long shadows.

How to Play:
1. Let one player from each team draw a word from the bag.
2. The members of the team use their bodies to make shadows of the letters.
3. The first player to correctly guess the word gets a point for his team.

Published by Frank Schaffer Publications.
Copyright protected.

0-7682-3412-3
101 Easy Reading Games

"BR" Cards

Used with Activities: 14, 43, 49, 53, 54, 72, 89, 100

brag	brain	brake	bran
branch	brand	brass	brat
brave	breath	bread	break
bride	brontosaurus	brook	broom
brother	brow	brown	brush

0-7682-3412-3
101 Easy Reading Games

dinosaur	opposite of *sister*	breakfast cereal	not afraid
used for sandwiches	sweeps the floor	makes hair look nice	to boast
person with no manners	comes from your lungs	a color	used for thinking
stops a bike	a small stream	used to build chimneys	part of a tree
over the eye	to tear apart	a shiny metal	it is done to cows

0-7682-3412-3
101 Easy Reading Games

"FR" Cards

Used with Activities: 15, 43, 49, 53, 54, 72, 89, 100

fraction	frame	Frank	freeze
freckles	free	freezer	fresh
fry	Friday	friend	fright
fringe	frizzy	frog	from
front	frost	frown	fruit

"GR" Cards

Used with Activities: 16, 28, 43, 49, 53, 54, 72, 89

grab	grade	graham cracker	grain
grandfather	grandmother	grape	graph
grasp	grass	grasshopper	gravy
gray	graze	great	green
greet	grip	grizzly	groom
ground	grow	growl	grunt

"TR" Cards

Used with Activities: 16, 28, 43, 49, 53, 54, 72, 74, 75, 89, 101

trace	track	tractor	trade
trail	train	tramp	trap
trash	travel	traffic	tray
treasure	treat	tree	trench
trend	trim	trip	tribe
trick	trumpet	truck	trust

"CR" Cards

Used with Activities: 16, 28, 43, 49, 53, 54, 72, 75, 89, 101

crab	crack	cradle	cramp
crane	crank	crash	crawl
crayon	cream	creek	creep
crib	cricket	crisp	crocodile
crook	cross	crow	crowd
crown	crust	crutch	cry

0-7682-3412-3
101 Easy Reading Games

"PL" Cards

Used with Activities: 16, 28, 43, 49, 53, 54, 72, 89

place	plaid	plain	plan
plane	plank	plant	plate
play	plead	please	pledge
plenty	plod	plot	plow
pluck	plug	plum	plus

0-7682-3412-3
101 Easy Reading Games

"SL" Cards

Used with Activities: 16, 28, 43, 49, 53, 54, 72, 89, 100

slam	slap	slave	sled
sleek	sleep	sleet	slice
slick	slide	slim	slime
slip	slob	slop	slope
slow	sloth	slug	sly

Published by Frank Schaffer Publications.
Copyright protected.

0-7682-3412-3
101 Easy Reading Games

"SM" and "SN" Cards

Used with Activities: 16, 28, 43, 49, 53, 54, 72, 89

smack	small	smash	smear
smell	smile	smirk	smooch
smooth	smudge	smug	snack
snag	snail	snake	snap
snare	snarl	snatch	sneak
sneer	sneeze	snicker	snip
snooze	snore	snort	snow

0-7682-3412-3
101 Easy Reading Games

"SK," "SP," "SQ," "ST," and "SW" Cards

Used with Activities: 28, 43, 49, 53, 54, 72, 73, 89

skate	skin	skinny	skip
skunk	space	speak	spell
spill	spin	spoil	spoke
spoon	sport	spot	squash
start	state	station	stay
square	squeeze	squirt	stale

store	step	stiff	still
stay	stock	steep	stall
sting	stomp	stare	study
stuff	swallow	swan	swap
sweet	swift	swim	swing
swam	sweep	swat	sway

"NG" Cards

Used with Activities: 16, 28, 43, 49, 53, 54, 72, 89

clang	cling	clung	slang
sling	wrong	spring	sprang
sprung	string	strong	strung
swing	swung	ring	rang
sting	stung	sang	sing
song	sung	long	among

Blend Word Family Cards

Used with Activities: 44, 67

__ace brace, grace, place, space, trace	__aid braid	__ain brain, drain, grain, plain, stain	__an bran, clan, plan
__ane crane, plane	__ank blank, clank, crank, drank, flank, frank, plank, prank, spank	__ant grant, plant, slant	__ate grate, plate, slate, state
__ay clay, gray, play, pray, slay, stay, sway	__ead bread, dread, tread, plead	__ease grease, please	__edge pledge
__enty plenty	__od clod, plod, prod	__ot blot, plot, slot, snot, spot, trot	__ow blow, crow, flow, glow, grow, slow, snow, stow, brow, plow
__ug plug, slug, smug, snug	__um drum, plum	__us plus	__oom bloom, groom, broom

Published by Frank Schaffer Publications.
Copyright protected.

0-7682-3412-3
101 Easy Reading Games

Number Word Cards

Used with Activities: 1, 17, 23, 45, 50, 53, 54, 89, 90

zero	one	two	three
four	five	six	seven
eight	nine	ten	eleven
twelve	thirteen	fourteen	fifteen
sixteen	seventeen	eighteen	nineteen
twenty	thirty	forty	fifty
sixty	seventy	eighty	ninety

Published by Frank Schaffer Publications.
Copyright protected.

0-7682-3412-3
101 Easy Reading Games

Animal Picture Cards

Used with Activities: 18, 24, 46, 50

Animal Picture Cards (cont.)

Published by Frank Schaffer Publications.
Copyright protected.

0-7682-3412-3
101 Easy Reading Games

Animal Word Cards

Used with Activities: 2, 18, 24, 35, 46, 50, 53, 54, 89, 90, 92

alligator	buffalo	butterfly	centipede
cheetah	cobra	coyote	crab
dragonfly	dinosaur	donkey	eagle
eel	elephant	gecko	giraffe
gorilla	hamster	hippopotamus	horse
jellyfish	kangaroo	kitten	lizard

Published by Frank Schaffer Publications.
0-7682-3412-3
101 Easy Reading Games

Animal Word Cards (cont.)

llama	monkey	moose	octopus
ostrich	platypus	pelican	penguin
quail	rabbit	rhinoceros	scorpion
sea horse	shark	slug	snake
snail	spider	squirrel	starfish
swine	turtle	whale	zebra

Published by Frank Schaffer Publications.
Copyright protected.

0-7682-3412-3
101 Easy Reading Games

Food Picture Cards

Used with Activities: 19, 25, 46, 50

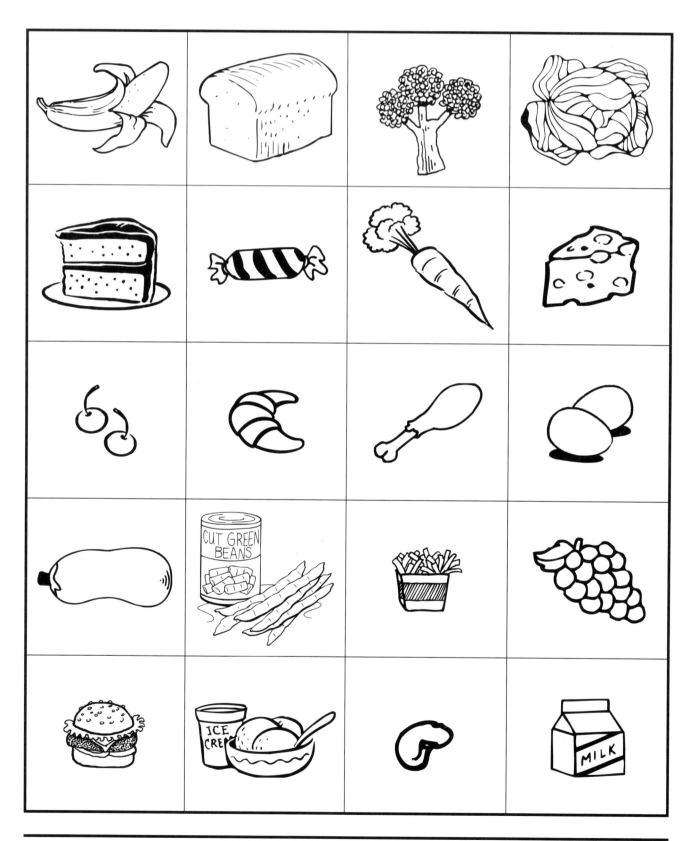

0-7682-3412-3
101 Easy Reading Games

Food Picture Cards (cont.)

Food Word Cards

Used with Activities: 2, 19, 25, 35, 46, 50, 53, 54, 89, 90, 92

bananas	bread	broccoli	cabbage
cake	candy	carrot	cheese
cherries	croissant	drumstick	eggs
eggplant	green beans	French fries	grapes
hamburger	ice cream	lima bean	milk

Published by Frank Schaffer Publications.

0-7682-3412-3
101 Easy Reading Games

Food Word Cards (cont.)

muffin	mushroom	pasta	peas
peanuts	pepper	pie	pineapple
pizza	popcorn	potato	pumpkin
sandwich	shrimp	soda	steak
strawberry	tea	tomato	zucchini

Published by Frank Schaffer Publications.
Copyright protected.

0-7682-3412-3
101 Easy Reading Games

Sight Word Cards

Used with Activities: 2, 20, 36, 43, 50, 53, 54, 70, 71, 77, 78, 79, 88, 93

about	afterward	against	always
anyone	around	because	been
before	best	better	both
bring	caller	came	carry
clean	cold	come	could
does	done	down	draw
drinking	everyone	falling	faster
finding	first	found	four
from	full	funny	gave

0-7682-3412-3
101 Easy Reading Games

Sight Word Cards (cont.)

give	goes	going	good
grow	have	help	here
him	holding	hurt	into
its	jumping	just	keep
kind	knew	knight	laugh
light	little	long	look
made	make	many	much
must	myself	never	new
nothing	now	off	older

Published by Frank Schaffer Publications.
Copyright protected.

0-7682-3412-3
101 Easy Reading Games

Sight Word Cards (cont.)

once	only	open	ourselves
out	over	own	player
please	pick	pretty	pulling
putting	read	right	round
said	seesaw	saying	seven
shall	she	show	sing
sleep	small	some	soon
start	student	take	teacher
thank	that	the	their

Published by Frank Schaffer Publications.
0-7682-3412-3
101 Easy Reading Games

Sight Word Cards (cont.)

them	then	there	these
they	think	this	today
together	tomorrow	try	under
upon	use	very	walk
want	warm	was	wash
well	went	were	what
when	where	willing	wish
with	worker	would	writer
yes	you	your	zoo

0-7682-3412-3
101 Easy Reading Games

Homophone Cards

Use with Activities: 21, 38, 51, 90, 91, 95

one the number between zero and two	**won** got first place	**our** belongs to us	**hour** 60 minutes
right correct	**write** record on paper	**peace** calm and quiet	**piece** part of something
too also	**two** the number between one and three	**rode** traveled in or on something	**road** street
see notice with your eyes	**sea** ocean	**blew** breathed hard on something	**blue** one of the primary colors
ant small insect	**aunt** the sister of a parent	**whole** the entire thing	**hole** an opening or pit
sent made something go	**cent** one penny	**flour** used to make bread	**flower** a pretty part of a plant

Published by Frank Schaffer Publications.

0-7682-3412-3
101 Easy Reading Games

Synonym Cards

Use with Activities: 4, 22, 27, 39, 47, 52, 90, 91, 96

small ———— little	near ———— close	last ———— final	leave ———— go	glad ———— happy
big ———— large	begin ———— start	above ———— over	damp ———— wet	rocks ———— stones
unhappy ———— sad	start ———— begin	scratchy ———— itchy	difficult ———— hard	gift ———— present
laugh ———— chuckle	talk ———— chat	hurry ———— rush	stop ———— end	task ———— job

Published by Frank Schaffer Publications.
Copyright protected.

0-7682-3412-3
101 Easy Reading Games

Antonym Cards

Use with Activities: 4, 22, 27, 40, 47, 52, 90, 91, 96

easy	tiny	lazy	insult	fancy
difficult	huge	helpful	compliment	plain
quick	tame	lock	raise	forget
slow	wild	unlock	lower	remember
everything	all	top	shout	brave
nothing	none	bottom	whisper	afraid
play	crooked	above	awake	early
work	straight	below	asleep	late

0-7682-3412-3
101 Easy Reading Games

Compound Word Cards

Use with Activities: 3, 21, 37, 90, 91, 94

baseball	swordfish	campfire	bookworm
meatball	starfish	fireplace	notebook
birthday	teaspoon	homesick	newspaper
daytime	teapot	homework	overcoat
footprint	skateboard	suitcase	fingernail
barefoot	snowboard	swimsuit	fingerprint

Published by Frank Schaffer Publications.
Copyright protected.

0-7682-3412-3
101 Easy Reading Games

Vocabulary Quiz Challenge

Use with Activities: 3, 4, 29, 48

Compound Word Riddles	Contractions	Antonyms	Synonyms	More Than 1
(1) Compound Word Riddles I am a sport that uses a bat. (baseball)	**(1) Contractions** What two words make up "didn't"? (did not)	**(1) Antonyms** The opposite of top. (bottom)	**(1) Synonyms** Another word for *near* is: a. far b. close (b. close)	**(1) More Than 1** man (men)
(2) Compound Word Riddles I am a sea animal shaped like something in the sky. (starfish)	**(2) Contractions** What two words make up "I'll"? (I will)	**(2) Antonyms** The opposite of crooked. (straight)	**(2) Synonyms** Another word for *happy* is: a. glad b. mad (a. glad)	**(2) More Than 1** mouse (mice)
(3) Compound Word Riddles I am a person who loves to read. (bookworm)	**(3) Contractions** What two words make up "here's"? (here is)	**(3) Antonyms** The opposite of forget. (remember)	**(3) Synonyms** Another word for *difficult* is: a. hard b. simple (a. hard)	**(3) More Than 1** tooth (teeth)
(4) Compound Word Riddles I am a natural disaster where the ground shakes. (earthquake)	**(4) Contractions** What two words make up "I'd"? (I would)	**(4) Antonyms** The opposite of wild. (tame)	**(4) Synonyms** Another word for *gift* is: a. present b. give (a. present)	**(4) More Than 1** child (children)
(5) Compound Word Riddles I keep a light bulb from being too bright. (lampshade)	**(5) Contractions** What two words make up "don't"? (do not)	**(5) Antonyms** The opposite of compliment. (insult)	**(5) Synonyms** Another word for *task* is: a. job b. take (a. job)	**(5) More Than 1** goose (geese)

Published by Frank Schaffer Publications.
Copyright protected.

0-7682-3412-3
101 Easy Reading Games

Homophone Quiz Challenge

Use with Activities: 4, 30, 48

Multiple Choice	Spell It	Define It	What Is This?	Write It
(1) Multiple Choice My team ____ the game! a. won b. one (a.)	**(1) Spell It** This is the number between one and three. (two)	**(1) Define It** hour: h-o-u-r (60 minutes)	**(1) What Is This?** 1 (one)	**(1) Write It** A *sea* is a large body of water. Write *sea*. (sea)
(2) Multiple Choice My hungry dog ate the ____ bone! a. hole b. whole (b.)	**(2) Spell It** notice with your eyes (see)	**(2) Define It** right: r-i-g-h-t (correct)	**(2) What Is This?** (ant)	**(2) Write It** A *hole* is an opening or pit. Write *hole*. (hole)
(3) Multiple Choice We all like ____ class pet. a. our b. hour (a.)	**(3) Spell It** breathed hard on something (blew)	**(3) Define It** too: t-o-o (also)	**(3) What Is This?** (flower)	**(3) Write It** *Blue* is one of the primary colors. Write *blue*. (blue)
(4) Multiple Choice Yesterday I ____ my bike all day. a. road b. rode (b.)	**(4) Spell It** the sister of a parent (aunt)	**(4) Define It** peace: p-e-a-c-e (calm and quiet)	**(4) What Is This?** (road)	**(4) Write It** You use *flour* to make bread. Write *flour*. (flour)
(5) Multiple Choice Jin wants to ____ a letter to Kelly. a. write b. right (a.)	**(5) Spell It** one part of something (piece)	**(5) Define It** sent: s-e-n-t (made something go)	**(5) What Is This?** (cent)	**(5) Write It** A *scent* is a smell. Write *scent*. (scent)

Published by Frank Schaffer Publications.
Copyright protected.

0-7682-3412-3
101 Easy Reading Games

Story Elements Quiz Challenge

Use with Activities: 32, 48

Character	Setting	Problem	Solution	Events
(1) Character Who is the main character in this story?	**(1) Setting** Where does this story take place?	**(1) Problem** What is the main problem in this story?	**(1) Solution** How is the main problem in this story solved?	**(1) Events** What happened in the beginning of this story?
(2) Character Name two other characters in this story.	**(2) Setting** When does this story take place?	**(2) Problem** Was there one problem in this story or more than one?	**(2) Solution** Was the main problem in this story solved on the first try?	**(2) Events** What happened in the middle of this story?
(3) Character Give two details describing the main character in this story.	**(3) Setting** In this story, was there one setting or more than one?	**(3) Problem** Name one character that had a problem in this story. Describe the problem.	**(3) Solution** How many times did the characters in this story try to solve the problem?	**(3) Events** What happened at the end of this story?
(4) Character Give four details describing one of the other characters in this story.	**(4) Setting** Give three details that describe the setting of this story.	**(4) Problem** Could the problem in this story really happen? Why or why not?	**(4) Solution** Could the main problem really be solved the way it is in this story? Why or why not?	**(4) Events** Could the events in this story really happen? Why or why not?
(5) Character Name a character from another story that is similar to a character in this story.	**(5) Setting** Name a story with a similar setting to the one in this story.	**(5) Problem** Name a story with a similar problem to the one in this story.	**(5) Solution** Name a story with a similar solution to the one in this story.	**(5) Events** Name a story with a similar sequence of events to those in this story.

Published by Frank Schaffer Publications.
Copyright protected.

0-7682-3412-3
101 Easy Reading Games

Fairy Tale Cards

Use with Activities: 32, 41

The Three Little Pigs	Goldilocks and the Three Bears	Cinderella	The Three Billy Goats Gruff
Sleeping Beauty	Snow White and the Seven Dwarfs	Hansel and Gretel	The Ugly Duckling
The Emperor's New Clothes	Pinocchio	Rumpelstiltskin	Chicken Little
The Little Red Hen	Little Red Riding Hood	The Boy Who Cried Wolf	The Tortoise and the Hare
The Little Mermaid	Beauty and the Beast	Jack and the Beanstalk	The Gingerbread Man

Published by Frank Schaffer Publications.

0-7682-3412-3
101 Easy Reading Games

Fairy Tale Quiz Challenge

Use with Activities: 33, 48

Characters	Setting	Name the Fairy Tale with This Problem	Name the Fairy Tale with This Solution	Lesson Learned
(1) Characters Who lived in a cottage with seven small men? (Snow White)	**(1) Setting** Which fairy tale took place in Never Never Land? (*Peter Pan*)	**(1) Problem** The main character lost his coat. ("Peter Rabbit")	**(1) Solution** Two characters moved in with their brother. ("The Three Little Pigs")	**(1) Lesson** Slow and steady wins the race. ("The Tortoise and the Hare")
(2) Characters Who never wanted to grow up? (*Peter Pan*)	**(2) Setting** Which fairy tale took place in a witch's house? ("Hansel and Gretel")	**(2) Problem** The main characters were lost and hungry. ("Hansel and Gretel")	**(2) Solution** The main character became a real boy. ("Pinocchio")	**(2) Lesson** Be kind, even to those who mistreat you. ("Cinderella")
(3) Characters Who climbed great heights to steal from a giant? (Jack in "Jack and the Beanstalk")	**(3) Setting** Name a fairy tale that took place in a castle. ("Sleeping Beauty," "Emperor's New Clothes," etc.)	**(3) Problem** The main character wanted to be a real boy. ("Pinocchio")	**(3) Solution** The characters found out the world wasn't ending. ("Chicken Little")	**(3) Lesson** Never go into the woods without a map. ("Hansel and Gretel")
(4) Characters Who discovered that you can't trust a wolf? (Gingerbread Man in "Little Red Riding Hood")	**(4) Setting** Name a fairy tale that took place in the woods. ("Little Red Riding Hood")	**(4) Problem** The main character got bored watching the sheep. ("The Boy Who Cried Wolf")	**(4) Solution** A lady figured out the character's mysterious name. ("Rumpelstiltskin")	**(4) Lesson** Beauty is in the eye of the beholder. ("Beauty and the Beast," "The Ugly Duckling")
(5) Characters She didn't respect other people's property. (Goldilocks)	**(5) Setting** Name a fairy tale that took place on a farm. ("The Little Red Hen")	**(5) Problem** The main character's friends were not helpful. ("The Little Red Hen")	**(5) Solution** The farmer and his wife had no dessert. ("The Gingerbread Man")	**(5) Lesson** If you lie, people won't trust what you say. ("The Boy Who Cried Wolf")

Published by Frank Schaffer Publications.

0-7682-3412-3
101 Easy Reading Games

What If Cards

Use with Activities: 7, 86

What if it rained root beer instead of water?	What if you saw a flying saucer and no one would believe you?
What if you had a tree that grew twenty dollar bills instead of leaves?	What if it rained all day and night for a week?
What if you found a diamond as big as your fist?	What if children could drive cars at age ten?
What if you could be president for a day?	What if you could fly an airplane?
What if you were the fastest runner in the world?	What if you could flap your arms and fly?
What if it snowed miniature marshmallows?	What if you were the strongest person alive?

Published by Frank Schaffer Publications.

0-7682-3412-3
101 Easy Reading Games

Cause and Effect Cards

Use with Activity: 7

The electricity went out. (C)	Mary's mother couldn't open the electric garage door. (E)	The batteries ran down in Mike's CD player. (C)	He had to buy new ones to make it work again. (E)
The wind blew the roof off Eric's house. (C)	Builders had to come out and put on a new one. (E)	Thunder woke the little girl who was afraid of the dark. (C)	Her mom turned on a night-light and tucked her back in bed. (E)
Someone ate Bret's lunch by mistake. (C)	He had to buy hot lunch instead. (E)	Parker found a five-dollar bill on the playground. (C)	He turned it in to his school's lost and found. (E)
Steven broke his thumb playing dodge ball. (C)	He had to wear a special splint on his hand. (E)	Sarah's father wouldn't let her go to the movies. (C)	She read a book instead. (E)
Amy ate too much pie. (C)	She got a terrible stomachache. (E)	Amaris forgot to close the freezer door. (C)	All the frozen food melted. (E)
James was afraid of the dark when the electricity went out. (C)	His mom lit candles to light up the house. (E)	Barbara played with matches. (C)	She burned her finger. (E)
Song Lee's dog was hit by a car. (C)	He had to go to the vet to get a cast on his leg. (E)	Mike got really angry and kicked his sister. (C)	He had to tell her he was sorry. He was also grounded for a week. (E)
Fredrico spilled ink on his new jacket. (C)	He took it to the dry cleaners to get out the spot. (E)	Paul ran across the street without looking for cars. (C)	A fast car almost hit him. (E)

Comprehension Quiz Challenge

Use with Activities: 10, 31, 42, 48

Classify: Which Doesn't Belong	Classify: Name This Group	Riddles (Conclusions)	Prediction	Cause & Effect
(1) Classify: Which Doesn't Belong? hat, doll, shirt, shorts (doll)	**(1) Classify: Name This Group** shark, tuna, goldfish (fish)	**(1) Riddles (Conclusions)** I am a big, green reptile with strong jaws. What am I? (alligator)	**(1) Prediction** What might happen on your next vacation? (answers vary)	**(1) Cause & Effect** The ground is slippery. What could have caused it? (ice, water, oil, etc.)
(2) Classify: Which Doesn't Belong? newspaper, CD, book, magazine (CD)	**(2) Classify: Name This Group** chair, couch, stool (things you can sit on)	**(2) Riddles (Conclusions)** I hop, have a pouch, and live in Australia. What am I? (kangaroo)	**(2) Prediction** What might happen next January? (answers vary)	**(2) Cause & Effect** The kitchen smells bad. What could have caused it? (rotting food, burned dinner, etc.)
(3) Classify: Which Doesn't Belong? ham, turkey, chicken, corn (corn)	**(3) Classify: Name This Group** Michigan, Texas, New York (states)	**(3) Riddles (Conclusions)** I am a huge brown animal with antlers. What am I? (moose)	**(3) Prediction** Zack accidentally broke his mom's picture. What might happen next? (answers vary)	**(3) Cause & Effect** Maria ate a whole tub of ice cream. What may be the effect? (stomachache, no appetite, etc.)
(4) Classify: Which Doesn't Belong? scissors, pen, marker, pencil (scissors)	**(4) Classify: Name This Group** hearing, taste, touch (senses)	**(4) Riddles (Conclusions)** My face looks like a horse. I am tiny and live in water. What am I? (sea horse)	**(4) Prediction** Liza just moved to a new school. What might she do next? (answers vary)	**(4) Cause & Effect** The lion escaped from his cage at the zoo. What will be the effect? (people running, closing the zoo)
(5) Classify: Which Doesn't Belong? can, bottle, knife, cup (knife)	**(5) Classify: Name This Group** elm, oak, pine (trees)	**(5) Riddles (Conclusions)** I am a bird, but I'd rather run than fly. What am I? (ostrich)	**(5) Prediction** Sara gave Jim a compliment. What might happen next? (answers vary)	**(5) Cause & Effect** Maya is angry. Name one cause and one effect. (answers vary)

Published by Frank Schaffer Publications.
Copyright protected.

0-7682-3412-3
101 Easy Reading Games

Skills Index
(Indexed by game number)

PHONEMIC AWARENESS
- Phonemes: 65

DECODING
- Final Blends and Digraphs
  CH and SH: 84
  NG: 16, 28, 43, 49, 53, 54, 72, 89
- Initial L Blends
  BL : 11, 44
  CL: 44, 99
  FL: 12, 44
  GL: 44, 82
  PL: 16, 28, 43, 44, 49, 53, 54, 72, 76, 89
  SL: 16, 28, 43, 44, 49, 53, 54, 72, 76, 89, 100
- Initial R Blends
  BR: 14, 43, 44, 49, 53, 54, 72, 76, 89, 100
  CR: 16, 28, 43, 44, 49, 53, 54, 72, 75, 89, 101
  DR: 44, 83
  FR: 15, 43, 44, 49, 53, 54, 72, 76, 89, 100
  GR: 16, 28, 43, 44, 49, 53, 54, 72, 76, 89
  PR: 44, 63
  TR: 16, 28, 43, 44, 49, 53, 54, 72, 74, 75, 89, 101
- Initial S Blends
  SM and SN: 16, 28, 43, 44, 49, 53, 54, 72, 76, 89
  SK, SP, SQ, ST, and SW: 16, 28, 43, 44, 49, 53, 72, 73, 76, 89
- Initial Varied Blends and Digraphs
  GN and QU : 61
  WH: 62
  SH: 13

- Long Vowels: 73
  Short Vowels: 66, 73
  Word Families: 44, 67

FLUENCY
- Word Fluency: 53, 70, 71

VOCABULARY
- Adjectives: 55, 56, 57, 58
- Animal Words: 2, 18, 24, 35, 46, 50, 53, 54, 89, 90, 92
- Antonyms: 4, 22, 27, 29, 40, 47, 52, 90, 91, 96
- Basic Sight Words: 2, 20, 26, 36, 43, 50, 53, 54, 70, 71, 77, 78, 79, 88, 93
- Contractions: 4, 29
- Compound Words: 3, 21, 29, 37, 90, 91, 94
- Food Words: 2, 19, 25, 35, 46, 50, 53, 54, 89, 90, 92
- Homophones: 4, 21, 30, 38, 51, 90, 91, 95
- Nouns: 55, 56, 57, 58
- Number Words: 1, 17, 23, 45, 50, 53, 54, 89, 90
- Plural Words: 4, 29, 48
- Synonyms: 4, 22, 27, 29, 39, 47, 48, 52, 90, 91, 96
- Verbs: 55, 56, 57, 58

COMPREHENSION
- Cause and Effect: 7, 10, 86
- Classifying: 10, 31, 35, 42, 69
- Drawing Conclusions: 10, 31, 42
- Fact and Opinion: 8, 80
- Fantasy and Reality: 9, 81
- Main Idea & Details: 10, 31, 35, 85
- Predicting: 31
- Sequencing: 87
- Story Structure: 6, 32, 33, 41, 9

0-7682-3412-3
101 Easy Reading Games